In Jesus' Name

In Jesus' Name

Johannine Prayer in Ethical, Missional,
and Eschatological Perspective

SCOTT ADAMS

Foreword by Jan van der Watt

☙PICKWICK *Publications* • Eugene, Oregon

IN JESUS' NAME
Johannine Prayer in Ethical, Missional, and Eschatological Perspective

Copyright © 2022 Scott Adams. All rights reserved. Except for brief quotations in critical publications or reviews, no part of this book may be reproduced in any manner without prior written permission from the publisher. Write: Permissions, Wipf and Stock Publishers, 199 W. 8th Ave., Suite 3, Eugene, OR 97401.

Pickwick Publications
An Imprint of Wipf and Stock Publishers
199 W. 8th Ave., Suite 3
Eugene, OR 97401

www.wipfandstock.com

PAPERBACK ISBN: 978-1-6667-3241-2
HARDCOVER ISBN: 978-1-6667-2609-1
EBOOK ISBN: 978-1-6667-2610-7

Cataloguing-in-Publication data:

Names: Adams, Scott [author]. | Van der Watt, Jan G [foreword writer]

Title: In Jesus' name : Johannine prayer in ethical, missional, and eschatological perspective / Scott Adams.

Description: Eugene, OR: Pickwick Publications, 2022 | Includes bibliographical references.

Identifiers: ISBN 978-1-6667-3241-2 (paperback) | ISBN 978-1-6667-2609-1 (hardcover) | ISBN 978-1-6667-2610-7 (ebook)

Subjects: LCSH: Bible—Prayers—History and criticism | Prayer—Biblical teaching | Bible—John—Criticism, interpretation, etc. | Bible—Epistles of John | Farewell Discourse | Bible—Revelation—Criticism, interpretation, etc.

Classification: BS2601 A33 2022 (print) | BS2601 (ebook)

Scripture quotations are taken from the ESV® Bible (The Holy Bible, English Standard Version®), copyright © 2001 by Crossway, a publishing ministry of Good News Publishers. Used by permission. All rights reserved.

Contents

Abbreviations vii

Foreword ix

Acknowledgements xiii

1. Introduction 1

2. Ethical and Missional Prayer in the Farewell Discourse 6

3. Ethical Prayer in 1 John 29

4. Missional Prayer in 3 John 44

5. Eschatological Prayer in Revelation 62

6. Contemporary Implications of Johannine Prayer 83

Bibliography 91

Abbreviations

General and Bibliographic

LXX	Septuagint
NT	New Testament
OT	Old Testament

Old Testament

Exod	Exodus
Lev	Leviticus
Num	Numbers
Deut	Deuteronomy
2 Sam	1 Samuel
2 Chr	1–2 Chronicles
Ps	Psalm
Isa	Isaiah
Jer	Jeremiah
Amos	Amos
Zeph	Zephaniah
Zech	Zechariah

New Testament

Matt	Matthew
Mark	Mark
Luke	Luke
John	John
Acts	Acts
Rom	Romans
1 Cor	1 Corinthians
2 Cor	2 Corinthians
Gal	Galatians
Eph	Ephesians
1 Thess	1 Thessalonians
Heb	Hebrews
Jas	James
1 Pet	1 Peter
2 Pet	2 Peter
1 John	1 John
Jude	Jude
Rev	Revelation

Deuterocanonical Works

4 Macc	4 Maccabees

Foreword

IN JESUS' NAME IS a timely book about prayer in the Johannine literature. It covers an important Johannine concept that has, strangely enough, not yet received any significant attention in scholarship. With this book, this particular lacuna in the scholarly literature is addressed. Dr. Scott Adams is also the ideal person for writing such a text, since he has been energetically engaged with this Johannine topic for several years, and over this period also published (*inter alia* his PhD) on aspects of prayer in John (see the bibliography).

In this book, Dr. Adams continues to develop the concept of prayer in Johannine literature, including analyses of the Letters of John and the Book of Revelation, consistently relating it to parts of the Gospel, like the Farewell Discourse, thus showing the conceptual interaction between all the Johannine documents, which in itself is valuable, not the least for determining the interrelation between the different Johannine documents. He interacts in honesty with the material, acknowledging differences, but also describing similarities without forcing the Johannine texts into one direction or the other.

With his further development of the concept of prayer, a broader perspective on prayer, as it is used by John, emerges, showing how the concept of prayer is applied in different situations and genres by the "Johannine circle." This enables Dr. Adams to describe the networking and interaction of prayer with ethical, eschatological, and missional perspectives. He further shows how prayer, as communication with God, has an impact on various aspects of life. His approach indeed leads to a rich reading experience, highlighting different dimensions of prayer.

Adams emphasizes that prayer is indeed performative as well as relational, influencing not only the actions and focus of the supplicants, but prayer also carries the conviction that it would influence those who are prayed for. It is done according to the will of God, which aligns the wishes of the supplicant with what pleases God. In this sense, God is always a co-participant in prayer, influencing the content of prayer. This has a profound influence on the attitude and behavior of the supplicants. Their prayers must pass the test of what pleases God. Apart from this, the focus of prayer on the well-being of others likewise highlights the purpose of Johannine prayer, aligning it not only with the love believers should have for one another, but also for advancing missionary activities. Believers should, for instance, pray for the restoration of fellow believers who violated God's ethical standards. He also shows how prayer in Revelation fulfills an eschatological role, representing a heavenly perspective on God's mission, dealing with the vindication of the martyrs, the final judgment, and the second coming of Jesus. These different perspectives not only show the situational relevance of prayer, but also the wide scope covered by the concept of prayer in John. Prayer should in no way be limited to the private requests of believers. It covers a much wider scope.

The analyses of the different relevant texts are based on a responsible exegetical approach and the application of sound interpretative principles that form part of his close reading of the Johannine texts. This allows the text to guide the interpretation and conclusions, without contaminating the reading process with ideas foreign to the Johannine text. Furthermore, Dr. Adams succeeds in presenting his "academic" materials in such a reader-friendly way that it would be accessible to a wider audience, including students and people who are not theologians yet are interested to learn more about prayer (in John). This means that readers can familiarize themselves with the topic by following his clear style and description of specific Johannine texts related to prayer.

Foreword

Of value is also the last chapter where Dr. Adams bridges the gap between the Johannine views about prayer and what believers could learn from that today. It is always a challenge to link the contextual message of the Bible with our current everyday lives, but he nevertheless shows how central aspects of Johannine prayer serve as meaningful guidelines for current-day believers. This ensures that this book is by no means a sterile academic reading of the Johannine text, but one that also has a message for believers today.

In Jesus' Name is a book that makes an important contribution to Johannine research, especially because it deals with material not previously related and discussed in this format. Not only the responsible examination of the texts, but also the scope of including the traditional Johannine literature (Gospel, Letters, and Revelation) in this analysis increase the value of this book. As an added bonus, the style and presentation of this work makes it a pleasure to read.

Professor Jan van der Watt (DD; DLitt; DTheol [h.c.])
Radboud University, the Netherlands

Acknowledgements

MY RESEARCH ON THE topic of Johannine prayer began in 2013 under the guidance of Dr. Jan van der Watt at Radboud University (Netherlands). Upon the successful defense of my dissertation in 2018, I published my work under the title, *Prayer in John's Farewell Discourse: An Exegetical Investigation*. However, my investigation was not complete. In the years that followed I sought to ascertain how prayer in the Farewell Discourse compares to prayer in 1 John, 3 John, and Revelation. I also sought to explore the ethical, missional, and eschatological implications of prayer within the Farewell Discourse and other Johannine documents. As with my PhD dissertation, I owe a great debt of gratitude to Dr. Jan for the insights and guidance he provided as I sought to bring the collective fruit of my research together in this book. I, among many, am thankful to be reaping in a field that he has labored in for decades. In particular, his work on Johannine ethics has shaped my thinking in notable ways. Therefore, it is an honor to stand on his scholarly shoulders as I further seek to bring clarity to the function of prayer in the Johannine literature.

Furthermore, it is necessary to offer a brief overview concerning the origination of the content of each chapter of this book.[1] The second chapter consists of my previously non-published work titled, "Ethical and Missional Prayer in John's Farewell Discourse." I want to extend my gratitude to Dr. Michael Gorman (St. Mary's Seminary and University) who reviewed this chapter and offered

---

1. Sources for the following articles appear in the bibliography at the end of this book.

ACKNOWLEDGEMENTS

several suggestions for improvement. The third chapter consists of my previously published article through *Neotestamentica* titled, "Prayer in Johannine Perspective: An Analysis of Prayer in the Farewell Discourse and 1 John." The fourth chapter consists of my previously published article through *Neotestamentica* titled, "An Examination of Prayer in 3 John 2 and the Farewell Discourse in Light of the Mission of God." The fifth chapter consists of my previously published article through *Neotestamentica* titled, "The Rhetorical Function of Petitionary Prayer in Revelation." Each of these published articles appears in this book in a slightly modified format. The sixth and final chapter contains my novel reflections concerning the contemporary implications of Johannine prayer. While more work needs to be performed, it is my hope that this work contributes in some manner to the ongoing scholarly discussion.

Soli Deo Gloria

Chapter 1

Introduction

A KEY FEATURE OF the Johannine literature is that God has uniquely revealed himself through Jesus Christ. As God's messenger to the world, Jesus makes the Father known through his words and his works. However, a cursory reading of the Johannine literature reveals that Johannine Christianity is not a one-way street; believers may, in turn, communicate with God through prayer in Jesus' name (John 14:13–14; 15:16; 16:23–24) and on the basis of his indwelling words (15:7). This privilege is especially relevant for the disciples in light of Jesus' departure to the Father (13:36; 14:1–3). Not only do they have direct access to communicate with God, they also have the ability to do so in a manner that contributes to the fruitfulness of the community of God and the advancement of the mission of God[1] in Jesus' physical absence. Thus, Johannine Christianity is best described as a two-way street of open communication with God.

This two-way paradigm is modeled by Jesus throughout the Fourth Gospel (hereafter FG) in numerous contexts (6:11; 11:41–42; 12:27–28; 17:1–26; 19:28, 30). The Father not only speaks to the Son, but the Son also speaks to the Father; and he always listens. In each example, the Evangelist provides the reader with a

---

1. Throughout this book the phrase "mission of God" refers to the Johannine community carrying forth and proclaiming the good news of Jesus' life, death, and resurrection to the world.

glimpse into the intimacy of the Father-Son relationship. Just as Jesus prayed to the Father with confidence knowing that his prayers were heard and would be attended to, so believers may pray to God with confidence knowing that they will have whatever they ask for insofar as they make their requests according to God's will (John 15:7; 1 John 5:14–15). As believers pray in Jesus' name, they will perform "greater works" and bear "much fruit" for the good of the world and for the glory of the Father (John 14:12–14; 15:5, 8, 16; see also 3 John 2). Accordingly, "the prayers of the saints" (Rev 5:8; 6:10; 8:3–4) that rise before God will result in acts of judgment and salvation that descend upon the earth. While prayer in the Farewell Discourse (hereafter FD) is offered for the continuation of God's mission, prayer in Revelation summons Jesus to come again in order to complete God's mission in the world (22:20). Thus, I would like to suggest that Johannine prayer has ethical, missional, and eschatological implications; and this book is dedicated to exploring such implications in light of the first-century Johannine community.

Rationale for and Overview of this Book

Over time notable works have been published that examine the topic of Christian prayer as it appears throughout the New Testament.[2] However, to my knowledge, no significant work has been published that identifies and traces the function of prayer as it appears throughout the FG, 1 John, 3 John, and Revelation, collectively. While many works examine prayer within each of these

---

2. For example, see Jeremias, *The Prayers of Jesus* (1967); Hunter, "The Prayers of Jesus in the Gospel of John" (1979); Bradshaw, *Daily Prayer in the Early Church* (1981); Charlesworth et al, *The Lord's Prayer and Other Prayer Texts from the Greco-Roman Era* (1994); Cullmann, *Das Gebet im Neuen Testament* (1997); Kiley et al, *Prayer from Alexander to Constantine* (1997); Karris, *Prayer and the New Testament* (2000); Longenecker, *Into God's Presence* (2001); Carson, *The Farewell Discourse and Final Prayer of Jesus* (1980); Ostmeyer, *Kommunikation mit Gott und Christus* (2006); Ostmeyer, "Prayer as Demarcation" (2009); Crump, *Knocking on Heaven's Door* (2006); Neyrey, *Give God the Glory* (2007).

INTRODUCTION

documents, I am not aware of any work that examines these documents in light of one another insofar as prayer is concerned. In my research of the topic of prayer I have discovered three functional implications to prayer in the Johannine literature, namely: (1) ethical, (2) missional, and (3) eschatological. Of course, at its very essence prayer is relational in nature. It is offered from a faithful relationship with God and assumes a faithful response from God. Notwithstanding, the Johannine documents link prayer to the ethical behaviors of the community, their missional responsibility to carry forth the message of Jesus into the world, and their eschatological impulse to call forth final outcomes upon their present situation. But what is the precise relationship between prayer and these topics? How does it function within this three-fold paradigm? These are some of the questions under examination in this book.

Through a close reading of the aforementioned texts in their final form, I will examine key prayer passages in these documents in order to form a holistic profile concerning the function of prayer across the Johannine tradition. Moreover, this study assumes that the FG was written first, followed by 1 John, 3 John, and then Revelation. It must be noted that I do not argue for common authorship, but rather I suggest that these documents emerged from a common tradition within the first-century Johannine community. As such, I will focus exclusively on this tradition without consideration to the wider Christian tradition within which it is situated. Of course, it would be beneficial to compare, contrast, and synthesize Johannine prayer with other Christian literature, but such an undertaking is well beyond the scope of this book.

At this point it is helpful to provide an overview of the general direction of this book as well as the specific aims of each subsequent chapter. Since I have examined the prayers of Jesus and the prayer in the FD at great length elsewhere,[3] I will not repeat my conclusions except when relevant to the present discussion. At various points throughout this book I will draw upon the descriptive prayers of Jesus and prescriptive prayer from the FD in order

---

3. Adams, *Prayer in John's Farewell Discourse*, 163–200.

to draw points of continuity within the Johannine prayer tradition as it is presented in 1 John, 3 John, and Revelation.

A more detailed summary of what follows in chapters 2–6 is as follows. In chapter 2 I examine John 14:13–14; 15:7; 16:23–24; and 17 for the purpose of discerning the ethical and missional implications of prayer within the FD. In particular, this chapter explores how Jesus' love-ethic (13:15, 34; 15:12–13) relates to prayer in his name and on the basis of his word(s) and commandment(s) (13:34; 14:13–15, 21; 15:7, 10–12). By considering the Decalogue as the possible implicit background to Jesus' commandment(s), this chapter shows how prayer in the FD is motivated by his loving, sacrificial example for the fruitfulness of the Johannine community (15:5, 8, 16) and for the salvation of the unbelieving world (3:16). In short, this chapter lays the ethical and missional foundation for the discussion that follows in subsequent chapters.

Chapter 3 analyzes the ethical implications of prayer in 1 John. In this chapter I argue that the author of 1 John wrote to expand the Johannine prayer tradition by addressing the relationship between ethical behavior and confidence in prayer (1 John 3:11–24). I also explore the link between prayer and the restoration of brothers and sisters within the community who had violated God's ethical standards (1 John 5:14–17).

Chapter 4 explores the meaning of *euchomai* ("pray") in 3 John 2 with respect to the success of the mission of God through the emissaries under Gaius's care. In this chapter I argue that *euchomai* likely involves *both* the Elder's wish for Gaius's overall well-being *and* his prayer that Gaius's prosperity would positively contribute to the mission of God. Moreover, this chapter shows how prayer in 3 John accords with the nature of petitionary prayer as it is prescribed in John chapters 14–16 and in the prayer of Jesus in chapter 17.

Chapter 5 examines petitionary prayer in Revelation 5:8; 6:10; 8:3–4; and 22:20 for the purpose of ascertaining its eschatological function. In this chapter I highlight the eschatological nature of petitionary prayer within Revelation as it relates to the completion of God's mission in the earth. In particular, I demonstrate that

INTRODUCTION

while prayer in the FD is prescribed from an earthly perspective for the continuation of God's mission in Jesus' absence, prayer in Revelation is described from a heavenly perspective[4] and is offered for the completion of God's mission as the martyrs are vindicated, the wicked are judged, and Jesus returns.

Chapter 6 explores the contemporary implications of Johannine prayer. As noted above, in many respects, this book is academic in nature and seeks to address critical questions that involve the nature and function of prayer within this narrower tradition. At the same time, this book also seeks to highlight key elements of Johannine prayer that are relevant to the contemporary reader who approaches the Scriptures not merely as ancient documents to be read and interpreted, but as timeless truths that are to be applied and obeyed. However, it must be noted that this final chapter will not offer fine points of application. Instead I will focus on specific principles that the reader can apply in his or her own life.

---

4. With the exception of Rev 22:20.

Chapter 2

Ethical and Missional Prayer in the Farewell Discourse

SCHOLARS HAVE DEVOTED A considerable amount of time discussing the topic of ethics in the FG. While many have noted the absence of explicit ethical imperatives within this document, others have successfully argued for a model that applies to the Johannine community and the unbelieving world. Notwithstanding, in spite of the scholarly strides that further clarify the nature of ethics and how they are expressed in the FG, little work has been performed that discusses the relationship between ethics and petitionary prayer in the FD in particular. Therefore, this chapter attempts to move the discussion forward by exploring how Jesus' love-ethic elucidates our understanding of prayer in his name and on the basis of his word(s) and commandment(s). With consideration to the Decalogue as the possible implicit background to Jesus' commandment(s), this analysis demonstrates how prayer in the FD is influenced by Jesus as the one to whom the Decalogue points and is therefore motivated by his loving example for the fruitfulness of the believing community and for the salvation of the world.

Ethical & Missional Prayer in the Farewell Discourse

Toward a Love-Ethic in the Fourth Gospel

It is widely recognized that the FG lacks the sort of moral teachings that are located within other New Testament documents.[1] There are no instructions concerning forgiveness (Matt 6:14–15), divorce (Mark 10:1–12), restitution (Luke 19:1–10), or how to handle sinful offenses (Matt 18:15–19). There is no Sermon on the Mount (Matt 5:1–7:27) or other ethical instructions such as those located in the Pauline literature (e.g., 1 Cor 13; Gal 5:16–26; 1 Thess 4:3–5). Accordingly, some scholars assert that the Christological emphasis of the FG has, to a certain extent, "crowded out" ethics within this document.[2] While some ethical principles can be established from the Johannine Christological profile, the reader is left with no explicit ethical directions or imperatives. In a rather harsh tone, Jack Sanders sets forth his belief concerning the so-called moral bankruptcy of Johannine ethics by writing,

> Johannine Christianity is interested only in whether he believes. "Are you saved, brother?" the Johannine Christian asks the man bleeding to death on the side of the road. "Are you concerned about your soul?" "Do you believe that Jesus is the one who came down from God?" "If you believe, you will have eternal life," promises the Johannine Christian, while the dying man's blood stains the ground.[3]

However, other scholars have sought to move the discussion forward by seeking to discern and defend the presence of implicit ethics within the Johannine literature.[4] In more recent times, a notable amount of discussion has centered on Jesus' love[5] commandment

---

1. For an overview of relevant scholarship concerning the so-called problem of Johannine ethics, see Skinner, "(How) Can We Talk about Johannine Ethics?," xvii–xix.

2. Hays, *The Moral Vision of the New Testament*, 140.

3. Sanders, *Ethics in the New Testament*, 100. Skinner also quotes Sanders in, "(How) Can We Talk about Johannine Ethics?," xxiv.

4. For the most thorough treatment to date, see Van der Watt and Zimmermann, *Rethinking the Ethics of John*.

5. In this analysis the term *love* is defined on the basis of its usage in the

as it is expressed in John 13:34, namely, "A new commandment I give to you, that you love one another: just as I have loved you, you also are to love one another" (see also 15:12–13).⁶ In this instance, Jesus provides a straightforward commandment that, in turn, has implications for believers and unbelievers alike.⁷ For example, Christopher Skinner has successfully demonstrated the universality and normativity of John's love command as it is expressed in the FD,⁸ and has done so by tracing the trajectory of love that begins with "one another" (13:34), moves toward "friends" (15:13–14), and culminates in Jesus' prayer for all believers (17:20).⁹ Skinner notes that the foot-washing episode (13:3–15) is a "symbolic act" that "anticipates Jesus' ultimate act of sacrificial self-giving—his death on behalf of the world."¹⁰ In washing the disciples' feet, Jesus provides an "example" (*hypodeigma*, 13:15)¹¹ that firmly elucidates

---

Johannine text. As will be seen below, such love does not center on human emotion but rather involves the (both human and divine) acts of giving, serving, and laying down one's life for others.

6. All Scripture quotations in this book are from the English Standard Version.

7. Michael Labahn is correct to note, "On one hand, the Gospel of John does not present a catalogue of prescribed actions and practical advice on how to deal with problems in everyday life. On the other hand, the Gospel calls for a basic love relationship within the social limits of the actual group to which it is addressed and narrates episodes that depict how one should and should not relate to the world inside and outside that group." Labahn, "'It's Only Love'—Is That All?," 41.

8. Skinner, "Love One Another," 25–42. Andreas Köstenberger sees the FD as the "epicenter of John's moral vision." Köstenberger, *A Theology of John's Gospel and Letters*, 521.

9. In Jesus' prayer (John 17) a clear trajectory is established that begins with those who believe and extends to those who will believe through the disciples who are sent. Jesus prays that the Father will keep his disciples in his name (v. 11), that they will have his joy fulfilled in themselves (v. 13), that they will be kept from the evil one (v. 15), that they would be sanctified in truth (v. 17). He further prays that future believers will be one (vv. 21, 23) and that they may be with him where he is to see his glory (v. 24). I will explore the ethical implications of chapter 17 in the final section of this chapter.

10. Skinner, "Love One Another," 31.

11. Moloney notes, "The choice of the Greek word 'example' (ὑπόδειγμα) continues the theme of self-gift in love, even to death." Moloney, *Love in the Gospel of John*, 106.

the nature of his love for his disciples and exemplifies the sort of love that his disciples are to display toward one another. However, in this paradigm Johannine love also contains missional implications. The aim is for the love within the believing community to capture the attention of the unbelieving world so that it will be drawn into the sphere of God's saving love through Jesus Christ.[12] Further, Michael Gorman says that John's Gospel "possesses an implicit love ethic, not merely of love toward outsiders generally, but of *enemy-love*."[13] He grounds this ethic in the incarnation of the *Logos* (1:1, 14) who became flesh in a hostile world in order to draw people into the loving union of the Father and Son. Following this paradigm, he sees *enemy-love* as further expressed in the "Son's similar sending of the disciples into the same hostile world with him as their example of love, and with the gift of God's shalom and God's Spirit to empower them."[14] While Skinner and other scholars have convincingly argued for a love-based ethic that has implications for believers and unbelievers alike, the analysis that follows will explore how this ethic relates to prayer within the believing community that the Evangelist addresses.

Ethical Prayer in Jesus' Name

As Jesus' final speech commences, the disciples find themselves situated in the midst of an eschatological crisis that, at first glance, seems to have little to do with ethics. Jesus' departure is close at hand, the disciples' hearts are troubled, and Jesus' mission appears to be incomplete.[15] However, as will be demonstrated below, the solution to this apparent crisis involves faithful disciples who offer ethical prayer for the honor of Jesus' name and the glory of

---

12. Skinner remarks, "Their [the disciples'] outward displays of love will have potentially universal implications, causing all to take notice." Skinner, "Love One Another," 33.

13. Gorman, "John's Implicit Ethic of Enemy-Love," 136.

14. Gorman, "John's Implicit Ethic of Enemy-Love," 136.

15. As I have argued elsewhere; see Adams, *Prayer in John's Farewell Discourse*, 201–2.

the Father. In John 14:12–14 the Evangelist provides the following paradigm for petitionary prayer.[16]

As seen in v. 12:

- Prerequisite: "Truly, truly, I say to you, whoever believes in me..."
- Privilege: "... will also do the works that I do; and greater works than these will he do..."
- Rationale: "... because I am going to the Father."

As seen in vv. 13–14:

- Privilege: "Whatever you ask in my name, this I will do...." "If you ask me anything in my name, I will do it."
- Rationale: "... that the Father may be glorified in the Son."[17]

In summary, the one who believes in Jesus will perform "greater works" than he performed for the purpose of the Father being glorified in the Son. The foundation of such works is Jesus' departure to the Father and prayer in Jesus' name. It is important to note that verse 12 highlights the works that believers will do. But verses 13–14 says that Jesus himself will do whatever believers ask in his name. In this model, prayer in Jesus' name eventuates Jesus performing his works through believers. As such, the specificity of prayer in Jesus' name and the results thereof are qualified by the nature of his person and work. The FG presents Jesus as the *Logos* who came from God as God (1:1) in order to take away the sin of the world (1:29).[18] Accordingly, the Johannine "I am" (*egō eimi*) statements with predicates (e.g., 6:35, 41, 48, 51; 8:12) and without (8:24, 28, 58; 13:19) find linguistic overlap with the divine phraseology employed in Exodus 3:14, Deuteronomy 32:39, and the "'I am'" sayings in Isaiah (e.g., 43:10, 25; 45:18–19; 46:4,

---

16. This is a slightly modified outline/paradigm from a previous article. See Adams, "Prayer in Johannine Perspective," 110–11.

17. See also John 15:16; 16:23–24.

18. For an analysis of Christological titles in the Johannine literature, see Stuhlmacher, *Biblical Theology of the New Testament*, 668–79.

9), which present Yahweh as the one and only savior of Israel. In unique attributive language, the Evangelist presents Jesus as the one and only divine Savior of the world (John 3:16).[19]

Prayer in Jesus' Name in Light of the Third Commandment

As might be expected, the novelty[20] of prayer in Jesus' name is not without theological complexity. Given the association between Yahweh and Jesus, praying in Jesus' name is inevitably analogous to taking up God's name and assuming the responsibilities thereof.[21] The seriousness of this task is recalled in the third commandment (Exod 20:7), which states, "You shall not take the name of the LORD your God in vain, for the LORD will not hold him guiltless who takes his name in vain." In the most basic sense, God's name (Yahweh) stands for his nature, essence, and corresponding matchless value.[22] Scholars have offered a number of interpretations and corresponding applications concerning this commandment. Most understand "misuse the name of the LORD" as involving specific prohibitions against perjury, trivial swearing, any use of the name in the service of untruth, and magical use of the name for evil

---

19. Additionally, Luke 2:21 indicates that the name "Jesus" (*Iēsous*) was given by the angel before Jesus' conception. The nature of his name and mission is elucidated in Matthew 1:21 wherein an angel of the Lord says to Joseph in a dream concerning the child of promise, "for he will save his people from their sins." The salvific nature of his mission is congruent with the accompanying name, "Immanuel" (Matt 1:23, "God with us").

20. Hurtado points out that "the ritual use of Jesus's name has no known parallel in Jewish tradition of the time.... Given that ancient Jewish tradition widely regarded God's name as sacred, this practice of invoking Jesus's name in prayer is momentous; Jewish opponents would likely have seen it as an unwarranted and dangerous innovation." Hurtado, *Lord Jesus Christ*, 390–91.

21. See also Stuhlmacher, *Biblical Theology of the New Testament*, 671.

22. Walter Kaiser notes, "'The name' of God stands for so much more than the mere pronouncing of his title of address. It includes: (1) his nature, being, and very person (Ps 20:1; Lk 24:47; Jn 1:12; cf. Rev 3:4), (2) his teaching or doctrine (Ps 22:22; Jn 17:6, 26), and (3) his moral and ethical teaching." Kaiser, "Exodus," 1:407.

purposes.²³ But Douglas Stuart is right in saying that "the commandment is worded generally enough to encompass any misuse of Yahweh's name—from making light of it or overtly mocking it, to speaking about Yahweh in any way disrespectfully, to using it as the theophoric element in a personal name under social pressure to have one's family 'look orthodox' when in fact their beliefs were pagan/idolatrous."²⁴ T. Desmond Alexander says further, "This would range from the most obvious breaches, such as blasphemy and taking false or unnecessary oaths, to actions such as wrongly declaring to speak in *YHWH*'s name or misrepresenting God's nature in conversation."²⁵ When violated, the commandment states that "for the LORD will not hold him guiltless who takes his name in vain." Once again, obedience to the third commandment involves acting and speaking in a manner that shows proper honor and respect to the one who issued it.²⁶

With this background in mind, scholars have provided a number of possible suggestions concerning the relationship between the Decalogue and the commandments in the FG. Jey Kanagaraj sees Jesus' words ("keep my commandments") as providing a key for understanding the implied ethics of the FG. He asserts that the Evangelist reflects on the Decalogue and reinterprets it through the person and work of Jesus.²⁷ In his view, the Decalogue may

---

23. Dozeman, *Commentary on Exodus*, 488.

24. Stuart, *Exodus*, 454.

25. Alexander, *Exodus*, 407.

26. C. H. Dodd says that knowing the name of God "is an expression which sums up the ideal attitude of Israel (or of the individual Israelite) to Jehovah." Dodd, *The Interpretation of the Fourth Gospel*, 93.

27. For a complete overview of his thesis, see Kanagaraj, "The Implied Ethics of the Fourth Gospel," 33-60. The terms *commandment* and *commandments* appear throughout the FG. The singular form appears in 10:18; 11:57; 12:49, 50; 13:34; 15:12. The plural form appears in 14:15, 21; 15:10 [*bis*]). Hays says concerning the latter, "There are repeated injunctions to the community to keep Jesus' commandments (14:15, 21; 15:10; cf. 1 John 2:3-6), but, remarkably, the actual content of these commandments is never spelled out in the text" (Hays, *The Moral Vision of the New Testament*, 138). Notwithstanding, it is likely that the plural form involves injunctions that further expand how love is expressed in the believing community.

in fact serve as the backdrop to the love-command in the FD.[28] Jan van der Watt suggests that the "full scope of the moral situation envisaged by the Decalogue is indeed present and addressed (except for the tenth commandment which is not explicitly dealt with)."[29] Although the Decalogue is not explicitly brought forth in the FG, it is nevertheless implicitly present in the narrative. As such, he sees various elements from the Gospel that have associations with the Decalogue.[30] For example, the Jews accuse Jesus of blasphemy (John 10:33), which relates to the honor of God as indicated in the first and third commandments. The exclusive worship of the one true God is also noted in the Gospel (4:23–24; 17:3). Jesus' cleansing of the temple (2:13–17) further reflects zeal for the honor of God and the nature of true worship. The topic of the Sabbath (e.g., 5:9–10; 7:22–24; 9:14–16) is a notable issue in the Gospel and coincides with the fourth commandment. The topic of murder appears (e.g., 5:18; 7:19) in several places in the Gospel, which has a clear link with the sixth commandment. The action of Judas in stealing money (12:6) relates to the eighth commandment. The ninth commandment pertains to bearing false witness, which is seen in Jesus' opponents' denial of the truth (8:48; 18:30; 19:7). While other examples can be cited, Van der Watt concludes by saying, "The Jewish law and tradition seem to be the moral bedrock of the value system in the Gospel. It seems fair to assume that the burden of proof rests with people who disagree to show that

---

28. Kanagaraj remarks, "The first Christians treated love as the summary of the Law (Rom. 13:8–10), the root of which, they rightly believed, goes back to Jesus himself (Mt. 22:35–40; Mk. 12:28–34; Lk. 10:26–28; cf. Lv. 18:5; 19:18). When they treated love for one's neighbour as fulfilment of the Law, they often understood 'Law' as pointing to the Decalogue (Rom. 13:9–10). A devout Jew would think of the Decalogue and other related moral precepts as fundamental to covenantal Judaism and the rendering of the love command in such negative as well as positive form is characteristically Jewish." Kanagaraj, "The Implied Ethics of the Fourth Gospel," 36.

29. Van der Watt, "Ethics and Ethos," 152.

30. The following sentences in this paragraph provide a summary of Van der Watt's research and conclusions. Van der Watt, "Ethics and Ethos," 153–54.

the intended context is not that of the Jewish law and tradition but some other moral context."[31]

Thus, although the third commandment is not explicitly repeated in the FG, the intent of the commandment is exemplified in the life and ministry of Jesus, who shows esteem for the one who issued the commandments, namely Yahweh.[32] For example, Jesus comes in his father's name (5:43) and performs his works in that name (10:25). In anticipation of his impending cross-death, Jesus prays, "Father, glorify your name." (12:28). He prays elsewhere: "I have manifested your name to the people whom you gave me out of the world" (17:6); "Holy Father, keep them in your name, which you have given me" (17:11); and "While I was with them, I kept them in your name, which you have given me" (17:12).[33] Larry Hurtado remarks concerning the implications of these examples,

> To speak of Jesus as invested with the divine name, as coming with and in the name of God, as given the name, and as manifesting God's name in his own words and actions, was to portray Jesus as bearing and exhibiting God in the most direct way possible in the conceptual categories available in the biblical tradition, and within the limitations of the monotheistic commitments of that tradition.[34]

Moreover, although Jesus bore God's name, he in turn prescribes prayer in his own name with the goal of the Father being glorified in him (14:13). In light of Jesus' divine self-identification and the Semitic etymology of his name, prayer in Jesus' name is analogous to prayer in Yahweh's name.[35] Since God has given his name to

31. Van der Watt, "Ethics and Ethos," 155.

32. For a helpful discussion on Jesus bearing the name of God, see Hurtado, *Lord Jesus Christ*, 381–85.

33. The Psalms in particular are replete with examples of regard for God's name (see Pss 5:1; 7:17; 8:1, 9; 9:2; 18:49; 20:7; 22:22; 23:3; 25:11; 29:2; 30:4; 33:21; 34:3; 44:8; 45:17; 52:9; 54:6; 61:8; 69:30, 36; 72:19; 75:1; 76:1; 83:18; 86:9; 86:11; 96:8; 97:12; 100:4; 103:1; 105:3; 106:8; 113:1–3; 115:1; 119:55, 132; 135:1, 3, 13; 138:2; 142:7; 145:1–2, 21; 148:5, 13; 149:3).

34. Hurtado, *Lord Jesus Christ*, 385.

35. Carmen Imes notes, "Jesus' prayer, 'hallowed be your name,' is not just

Jesus, and Jesus is Yahweh's saving envoy to the world, then Jesus' name must be utilized in a manner that coheres with the intent of the third commandment.[36] Carmen Imes says, "The name of God is not a charm to be used at will. Those who fail to carry out God's will bear his name in vain."[37] As such, Jesus' name should never be utilized to coerce God[38] or offered in a flippant, irreverent manner. It should never be employed for selfish gain or self-seeking purposes.[39] It should be honored, esteemed, and always employed in an ethical manner that coheres with his nature and mission. It is not offered solely for the benefit of the worshiper, but for the glory of God and advancement of his cause. In this understanding, Johannine prayer is ethical insofar as it seeks to show proper reverence for the giver of the Law and the one to whom it points (God and Jesus).

Prayer in Jesus' Name as the Continuation of Jesus' Works

Further, the Evangelist indicates that the Father is glorified in the Son as prayers are answered and greater works are performed in Jesus' name. As the divine envoy, Jesus does nothing out of his own will (5:30) but only does (or imitates) what the Father is doing (5:19; 10:25, 37–38; 14:10, 31). Correspondingly, disciples who

---

wishful thinking, as though Jesus is hoping that Yahweh is doing well up there. His prayer implies a personal commitment to honoring that name through a life of faithful obedience. He fulfills Israel's vocation to bear Yahweh's name with honor." Imes, *Bearing God's Name*, 138.

36. Brown, *The Gospel according to John*, 536.

37. Imes, *Bearing God's Name*, 138.

38. James Jeffers says about Greco-Roman prayer, "There arose a body of rules telling what had to be done or avoided in order to influence the gods for good. These rules were not a code of behavior, but governed the proper performance of rituals, such as how to say a blessing or sacrifice an animal . . . in essence prayer was an attempt to coerce the forces of nature." Jeffers, *The Greco-Roman World*, 90.

39. Naomi Janowitz says that, "'Magic' was not bad because it was fraudulent . . . in the main magic was dangerous because it *worked*." Janowitz, *Magic in the Roman World*, 3. For an overview and analysis of magic in Greek and Greco-Roman prayer, see Klauck, *The Religious Context of Early Christianity*.

have faith in Jesus and offer petitions in his name will imitate him (and the Father) by performing greater works that have soteriological outcomes.[40] Such works are greater because they make Jesus known to the world in light of his finished work and departure to the Father (14:12; 19:30; 20:17). In this understanding, their works effectively carry forth the salvific mission of God into the world with evangelistic success. Again, it must be noted that the disciples' works are not exclusively their own; on the contrary, as they pray in Jesus' name, Jesus himself will do whatever they ask.

Thus, even after his departure to the Father, Jesus continues to bring glory to the Father by working through disciples who stand in faithful union with him. In light of his glorification, disciples may approach the Father directly[41] in Jesus' name and he will answer their prayers so that their joy will be full (16:23–24). Such joy is in response to answered prayer[42] as more and more people believe that Jesus is the Christ, the Son of God (20:31).[43] With Jesus' example in mind (13:15; 13:34), it is plausible to suggest that prayer in Jesus' name might naturally be viewed as prayer that imitates his loving example as set forth in the foot-washing episode and in his cross-death for the sake of the world (3:16).[44]

40. F. F. Bruce writes, "In the first few months after His death and resurrection many more men and women became followers through their witness than had done so during His personal ministry in Galilee and Judea." Bruce, *The Gospel and Epistles of John*, 300. Alan Culpepper notes similarly, "The future works will be greater not because they will be better or more spectacular, but because they will be more extensive (the mission and spread of the church)." Culpepper, *The Gospel and Letters of John*, 211. Rudolf Schnackenburg sees "greater works" as "the missionary success of the disciples." Schnackenburg, *The Gospel according to St. John*, 72.

41. See Karl-Heinrich Ostmeyer, who examines the usage of *erōtaō* and *aiteō* with respect to prayers offered by Jesus and the disciples, respectively. Ostmeyer, "Prayer as Demarcation," 242–47.

42. In this instance, it is the Father who answers prayer.

43. Paul Rainbow notes, "Fruits of evangelization are greater, to the extent that the life of the age to come is of a higher order than that of the present age." Rainbow, *Johannine Theology*," 411.

44. Karl Weyer-Menkhoff says that the Father has "set up a pathos to which Jesus should respond. Now Jesus defines his actions as pathos that is to be responded to by the believers." Weyer-Menkhoff, "The Response of Jesus," 165.

In particular, the foundation of the disciples' communal and soteriological *praxis* is a love-based example that provides the content and contours of their prayers. In this model, Johannine prayer is motivated by esteem for Jesus' name and all that his name represents. This sort of prayer is ethical because it not only seeks for welfare of the believing community, but it also longs for the salvation of the world. It is offered from the disciples' relationship with Jesus, but it also seeks for others to be drawn into relationship with the Father through him (14:6).

Prayer in Jesus' Name for the Honor of the Father

As greater works are performed, the Father is glorified in the Son (14:12-13). The theme of God's glory/honor is not addressed further in John 14, but it is picked up again in Jesus' discussion of answered prayed and the results thereof in 15:7-8. In these instances, the disciples are commissioned to pray (presumably) as members of the family of God in a manner that upholds the reputation of their Father. As new members are added to the family, they necessarily assume a new identity and their ethical choices must reflect this identity.[45] Jerome Neyrey and Eric Stewart note, "In antiquity a person is primarily known as the 'son of So-and-So' or the 'daughter of So-and-So.' Identity and honor derive in large part from membership in a family or clan. . . . To know a person, ancient peoples thought it essential to know that person's bloodlines."[46] Therefore, the children of God must live in accordance to the spiritual bloodline and ethical value system of their Father (1:12-13). While the glory of the Father is the aim of Jesus' overall ministry (7:18; 11:4; 13:31-32), this pursuit is exemplified in several instances that directly involve Jesus' relationship with the Father and his prayers to him. For example, Jesus gives thanks for the loaves and fish, and does so (presumably) in honor of the Father (6:11). Jesus says to Martha before his prayer to the Father

---

45. For an overview of the familial imagery and metaphors in the FG, see Van der Watt, *Family of the King*, 307-20.

46. Neyrey and Stewart, *The Social World of the New Testament*, 89-90.

at the tomb of Lazarus, "Did I not tell you that if you believed you would see the glory of God?" (11:40); He prays in 17:4, "I glorified you on earth, having accomplished the work that you gave me to do." Finally, just before his death Jesus says, "It is finished" (*Tetelestai*), which serves as a prayer of finality concerning the work the Father gave him (19:30).[47] In this instance, the Father is glorified by Jesus' perdurable obedience to the will of the Father to the point of death.[48]

These examples provide a didactic model that believers may imitate as they seek to pray in a manner that honors the Father. While the Evangelist does not enunciate the exact content of prayer in the FD, the emphasis placed upon the Father's glory/honor requires that it conforms to the family values established by the Father and modeled by Jesus' loving example. Prayer for other purposes is a betrayal of the ethical standards of the family. As Jesus did nothing of his own, disciples should never offer petitions based on motivations that are incongruent with or antithetical to the will of God as expressed through Jesus.

Ethical Prayer according to Jesus' Words

In 15:1–8 the Evangelist describes relationship with Jesus in agrarian terms (e.g., vine, vinedresser, branches). As disciples abide in Jesus, the vine, they are granted the privilege of asking for whatever they wish and it will be done for them. Once again, the Evangelist provides a prerequisite/privilege/purpose/result paradigm in the following verses.[49]

---

47. Stuhlmacher, *Biblical Theology of the New Testament*, 690–91.

48. Van der Watt remarks further, "Jesus is sure that the Father will always hear his prayers (11:41–42; see also 11:22) and he therefore communicates freely with the Father (ch. 17; 14:16). They stand in a relationship characterized by intimate knowledge (17:25). Jesus therefore prays for Lazarus (11:41–42), but also for his disciples (14:16; 16:26; 17:1–26). In both cases Jesus pleads for their welfare according to the will and glory of the Father." Van der Watt, *Family of the King*, 228.

49. As outlined in my previous work, Adams, "Prayer in Johannine Perspective," 111.

As seen in v. 7:

- Prerequisite: "If you abide in me, and my words abide in you."
- Privilege: "Ask whatever you wish, and it will be done for you."

As seen in v. 8:

- Purpose and Result: "By this my Father is glorified, that you bear much fruit and so prove to be my disciples."

In summary, disciples who abide in relationship with Jesus and allow Jesus' words to abide in them will bear much fruit (vv. 5, 8) that brings glory to the Father. In this model, the Evangelist links faithfulness to moral and missional fruitfulness. Jesus' words collectively constitute his "word" (15:3), which inevitably consist of his individual utterances that were spoken gradually over the course of his ministry and were later recalled by the Evangelist and the Johannine community. Daniel Stevick remarks, "The language suggests that Jesus' remembered words were an informing, regulative presence among Jesus' followers and in their life of asking.... Where his words abide, the person whose words they are abides."[50] At first glance, Jesus' call for the disciples to abide in him and for his words to abide in them (15:7) may have little to do with ethics. However, as will be discussed below, the Evangelist indicates that all that Jesus says and does flows from his union with and education from the Father. From this union Jesus speaks only what he hears from the Father (8:38; 12:49–50). Thus, if it can be maintained that Jesus' words include all that he spoke during his ministry, and if all that Jesus spoke was true[51] and in obedience to the will of his father who is the "sole determiner of right and wrong,"[52] then, by extension, the sum total of his words provides a Christological profile with ethical implications.

---

50. Stevick, *Jesus and His Own*, 203.

51. In the FG the term *alētheia* appears in 1:14, 17; 3:21; 4:23, 24; 5:33; 8:32, 40, 44 (*bis*), 45, 46; 14:6, 17; 15:26; 16:7, 13; 17:17, 19; 18:37, 38.

52. As noted by Van der Watt, *Family of the King*, 214.

In Jesus' Name

Prayer according to Ethical Education

Van der Watt has written extensively on the theme of education within the family of God. In particular, he sees John 5:17–30 as effectively describing Jesus' education from the Father.[53] Jesus says in 5:19, "Truly, truly, I say to you, the Son can do nothing of his own accord, but only what he sees the Father doing. For whatever the Father does, that the Son does likewise." He remarks further in verse 20, "For the Father loves the Son and shows him all that he himself is doing." In this model the Father is presented as the representative who performs actions and words for Jesus, the receiver. In turn, Jesus watches, sees, hears, learns, and copies. In particular, the Father's work involves raising people from the dead, giving them life, and judging them (5:21–22; 26–27). In turn, Jesus gives life to whomever he wishes (5:21). Accordingly, in John 7:16 Jesus says that his teaching is not his own, but his who sent him. In John 8:28 Jesus remarks that he does nothing on his own, but he speaks what the Father has taught him. In turn Jesus educates disciples who abide in his word (8:31). He makes the Father known (1:18), and does so through his words and works. As noted above, in John 13:2–15 Jesus provides a concrete example of love and humility in the foot-washing episode.[54] As their teacher (13:13), Jesus provides ethical education to his disciples by his actions and then iterates the necessity of replicating it in their love for one another (13:34–35; 15:12–14, 17). As they are obedient to the education they received, the disciples confirm their status as Jesus' friends and receive further insider revelation on the basis of this friendship (15:14–15). As will be discussed below, when Jesus' words are received, adhered to, and obeyed (5:24; 6:60; 12:47; 15:7), they inevitably have a transforming effect on the ethical value system of the believer in general and his or her prayers in particular.

---

53. This entire paragraph is a summary of Van der Watt's research and conclusions (Van der Watt, *Family of the King*, 215–23).

54. See also John 10:11–18; 19:16–30.

To summarize, Jesus provides an education[55] from above for his disciples below through his deeds and utterances. Although his works, word(s), and commandment(s) are not explicitly drawn from the Decalogue, they are congruent with the intent of the Decalogue, namely love for Yahweh and others.[56] In this model, Jesus is the ultimate basis for ethics. Raymond Brown reminds the reader that the Decalogue is set within the context of God's covenant with Israel at Sinai.[57] By observing his commandments, the people of God were thus identified as his covenant people. He goes on to argue that by speaking of the new commandment of love as the distinguishing feature of the disciples, the Evangelist implicitly shows the Last Supper in covenant terms. In this understanding, Jesus initiates a new covenant characterized by a love-ethic that is uniquely exemplified through his example of servanthood. Therefore, praying on the basis of one's union with him not only involves making petitions according to the motivation of love as assumed in the Decalogue, but it involves making requests on the basis of Jesus' words and example (John 13:15; 34).[58]

---

55. It must be noted that the standards of the community cannot be reduced to a crystalized set of rules, but, as indicated by Van der Watt, involve "the attitude and behavior of Jesus, actualized in believers through the Spirit (14.15–19; 15.26–27; 16.5–16; 1 Jn 2.20, 27; 3.24), that serve as an ethical guideline." Van der Watt, *An Introduction*, 60.

56. William Loader says, "[I] want to emphasize that we should expect the community to remain wedded to many of the values and traditions of the Torah, even if ideologically it is no longer the alleged basis for ethics." In this understanding, placing Christ in place of the Torah was not the abandonment of the Torah or the God who gave it, but instead was "truly following where they allege it led." Loader, "The Law and Ethics in John's Gospel," 157–58.

57. Brown, *The Gospel according to John*, 612.

58. Craig Koester notes, "Jesus claims to communicate what he received directly from God. He does so in a manner that is not derived from the law and yet is congruent with the law (5.39–47; 7.14–18). So when asking, 'What should I do?', the Fourth Evangelist's response would be 'Follow Jesus.'" Koester, "Rethinking the Ethics of John," 92.

In Jesus' Name

Prayer for the Fruitfulness of the Community

Prayer according to Jesus' words and example aims for the glory of the Father, but it also, by necessity, seeks for the welfare of the family of God and its numerical growth. Accordingly, such prayer seeks God's glory above all things and maintains high regard for his name (Exod 20:7). It values truth over falsehood and is offered for the well-being of others in the community. It promotes honor over dishonor (Exod 20:12), life over death (Exod 20:13), and contentment over covetousness (Exod 20:17). It seeks for the well-being of insiders within the family of God, but also longs for outsiders to be drawn into relationship with the true God of Israel through Jesus.

Thus, the agrarian language of John 15 contains communal and missional implications for the believing community. In particular, as the disciples remain in relationship with Jesus, the vine, and pray according to his words (15:1–7), they have the potential to bear "much fruit" for the glory of the Father (15:8). Such disciples will bear "fruit" that "abides" as they offer prayer to the Father in Jesus' name (15:16). The term *fruit* (*karpos*) appears in numerous places throughout the FG (4:36; 12:24; 15:2, 4, 5, 8, 16). In the context of chapter 15, fruit is the by-product of living in union with Jesus and being obedient to his commandment(s).[59] As the disciples are faithful to Jesus and pray according to his indwelling words, his loving character and values are replicated through them as they love one another and produce more disciples who do the same (hence, "much fruit"). As fruit is produced, the ethical values from above are displayed within the Johannine community below and God's saving mission is carried forth. Failure to bear the fruit of love within the community will undermine the evangelistic mission of God and the efficacy of the disciples' witness to the world.

---

59. Carson, *The Gospel according to John*, 517, 523.

Ethical Prayer in a Hostile World

While love for God and one another qualifies the nature and outcome of prayer within the believing community, love for the world provides motivation for the disciples' ministry to those outside the community.[60] In 15:18—16:4, the Evangelist highlights the world's hatred of Jesus, and by extension, its hatred of believing disciples who abide in relationship with him. This raises the question concerning how Jesus-followers are to pray in the face of community conflict and worldly hostility. More specifically, what is the nature of their prayers toward outsiders? In contradistinction to the Psalms[61] and Revelation,[62] prayer in the FD contains no trace of imprecation or pleas for vengeance. As will be argued in chapter 5, prayer in the FD is offered from an earthly perspective for the continuation of God's mission, whereas prayer in Revelation is offered from a heavenly perspective (Rev 5:8; 8:3–4) for the completion of God's mission through acts of salvation and judgment. The former is offered in light of Jesus' departure, whereas the latter summons his return (Rev 22:20). As the FD unfolds, the Evangelist simply repeats the necessity of praying in Jesus' name (John 16:23–24) without additional qualification, which most plausibly centers on prayer for the success of God's salvific mission in the world. In this model, the disciples' love is turned inside out for the good of the world that stands in opposition to it. Labahn says concerning this love/hate paradigm, "The community is loved by the God who loves the world (John 3:16) but hated by the world that does not acknowledge the Johannine discourse narrative. In such a context, group members are asked to take a certain responsibility for the world outside."[63] Richard Hays remarks further, "Even though their primary mandate is to manifest love and service within the community, the disciples who share Jesus' mission in the world

---

60. For discussion concerning the implications of the new commandment, see Labahn, "'It's Only Love'—Is That All?," 21–22.

61. See, for example, Pss 5, 10, 17, 35, 38, 58, 59, 70, 109, 129, 137.

62. See Rev 6:9–11; 8:3–4.

63. Labahn, "'It's Only Love'—Is That All?," 42.

can hardly remain indifferent to those outside the community of faith."[64] From the standpoint of the FD, prayer in Jesus' name and on the basis of his words/commandments serves as one of the means by which group members take responsibility for the community they participate in and for the world they seek to reach.[65] As Jesus laid his life down for the disciples and the world (3:16), so those who pray in his name must be willing to lay down their lives for the sake of God's saving mission in the world. As noted by Van der Watt, believers have a "soteriological agenda" like the Father who loves the world.[66] In the final analysis, prayer according to Jesus' love-ethic serves as one of the means by which individuals in the world become the friends of Jesus and members of the community of God.

The Ethical Implications of Jesus' Prayer (John 17)

Until this point, the focus of this chapter has centered on the nature of the disciples' prayer to Jesus/Father. However, I will conclude by briefly exploring the ethical implications of Jesus' prayer in John 17. Situated at the end of the FD, the Evangelist records the lengthiest prayer in the Gospel tradition wherein Jesus presents a status report[67] concerning the completion of his mission and prays for his disciples (vv. 6–19) and all who will believe in him (vv. 20–26). In this prayer the Evangelist picks up themes that appear in the Book of Signs and the FD in particular including the glorification of the Son, Jesus' departure to the Father, the oneness of the Father and Son, and persecution from the world.[68] As the prayer begins, Jesus says, "Father, the hour has come; glorify your

---

64. Hays, *The Moral Vision of the New Testament*, 145.

65. Koester says, "If the followers of Jesus are to act in ways congruent with what God has done, then their witness to the world must attest to God's love for the world. A purely sectarian form of love would not do so." Koester, "Rethinking the Ethics of John," 89.

66. Van der Watt, *An Introduction*, 63.

67. For further discussion, see Van der Watt, *An Introduction*, 43.

68. Skinner, "Love One Another," 36.

Son that the Son may glorify you" (v. 1; see also v. 5). Jesus then indicates that he glorified the Father by accomplishing the work the Father gave him to do (v. 4), manifested the Father's name to those whom he gave him out of the world (vv. 6, 26), gave them the Father's word(s) (vv. 8, 14), and kept them in the Father's name (v. 12). Accordingly, he prays that his followers will be kept in the Father's name (v. 11), kept from the evil one (v. 15), and sanctified in truth (v. 17), and that those who will believe in him will become one as he and the Father are one (vv. 20–23). The pinnacle of this prayer begins in verse 25 wherein Jesus affirms his knowledge of the Father ("I know you") and reaches its final peak in verse 26 as Jesus declares, "I made known to them your name, and I will continue to make it known, that the love with which you have loved me may be in them, and I in them."

With this brief overview in mind, there are several aspects of this prayer that have ethical implications for the believing community and the unbelieving world. Jesus prays, "Holy Father, keep them in your name, which you have given me, that they may be one, even as we are one" (v. 11). Since the Father has given his name to Jesus, then being kept in the Father's name is synonymous with being kept in Jesus' name and the revelation he embodied. The aim of being kept in this manner centers on the disciples being one just as (*kathōs*) Jesus and the Father are one (also vv. 20–23). This outcome of this petition stands in sharp contrast to the "son of destruction," who was lost in order that the Scriptures might be fulfilled (v. 12). In ethical terms, Judas was not only a thief, but he also betrayed Jesus and the value system he embodied (12:4–6; 13:2, 26–26). Thus, for the Johannine Jesus, being kept in the Father's name inevitably involves being kept in relationship with Jesus and being preserved in the ethical values disclosed through his words and works. Further, in 17:15 Jesus asks the Father to "keep" the disciples from "the evil one." In one reading, Jesus prays that his followers will be kept from evil (in the abstract).[69] In another reading, the evil one is the devil who is elsewhere presented as a

---

69. For further discussion, see Carson, *The Gospel according to John*, 565.

murderer and the father of lies (8:44).[70] In my view, Jesus is not merely asking that his followers be kept from evil in general, but that they be kept from the devil's unethical influence in particular.

Accordingly, Jesus prays that they will be "sanctified" in the "truth" (17:17), which involves (in part) the disciples adhering to the ethical education they received from the Father (v. 25, the vocative, *Patēr dikaios*) through Jesus' word(s) and commandment(s). As noted by Brown, "In common Jewish prayer . . . it was proclaimed that God sanctifies (consecrates) men through His commandments—an idea that is partially similar to John's thought, since for John 'word' and 'commandment' are virtually interchangeable."[71] In the Johannine model, one's education is either from the Father above or from the devil and his children below (8:44). It consists of either truth or falsehood, righteousness or unrighteousness, ethical or unethical values. There is no middle ground. Therefore, as Jesus was consecrated[72] in the world (v. 19), so those who follow him must be ethically distinct from the world. Since Jesus is the truth (14:6), so his followers must live according to that truth. Once again, as this occurs the believing community reflects the ethical value system of the Father and Son in the unbelieving world.

Finally, in 17:20–21 Jesus prays that future believers will be one, and that on the basis of their oneness the world will believe that the Father sent him. Such unity is likened to the Father-Son model of mutual indwelling (v. 21, "just as you, Father, are in me, and I am in you"). From this divine union Jesus gives believers the "glory" (*doxa*) he received from the Father that they may be one as he and the Father are one (v. 22). And from this divine union believers are to be "perfectly one" so that the world will know that the Father sent Jesus and loves them deeply even as (*kathōs*) he loved Jesus (v. 23). Jesus says more explicitly, "the love you have for me may be in them" (v. 26). Correspondingly, the same love that is "in them" will reach beyond them as they seek to advance God's saving

---

70. See John 12:31; 14:30; 16:11 as references to "the rule of this world."
71. Brown, *The Gospel according to John*, 765.
72. See Lev 11:44–45; 1 Pet 1:16.

mission in the world. Gorman says, "Loving one another does not require the disciples to go anywhere, but loving a hostile world certainly does (15:16, 'go'). Thus, Jesus' love command and example do not end with love among the disciples, nor do they have internal unity as their ultimate goal. Such love and unity are meant to bring others into the divine love and life."[73] In this paradigm, the love and unity of the believing community has a "missionary consequence" that is patterned after the Father-Son relationship.[74] In ethical terms, as believers abide in Jesus and imitate his example, the love expressed within the believing community will be turned inside out for the sake of the unbelieving world.

Conclusion

Recent scholarship has successfully elucidated the presence of a *communal and missional* model of Johannine ethics. Building upon this foundation, this chapter has sought to move the discussion forward by exploring the relationship between ethics and petitionary prayer in the FD. My research reveals that, while the FD contains no explicit ethical guidelines for petitionary prayer, it does provide a Christological profile that inevitably contains ethical implications for prayer. Kanagaraj is correct in saying that it is "in Christ that the character of God is revealed and that people can clearly see what the right things are and how to do them."[75] This is most certainly the case with respect to petitionary prayer. By considering the Decalogue as the possible implicit background to Jesus' commandment(s), this analysis has shown that prayer in the FD is modeled after Jesus as the one to whom the Decalogue points and is therefore motivated by his loving example for the fruitfulness of the believing community and for the salvation of the unbelieving world. Those who follow Jesus' example and pray in his name and on the basis of his words will offer ethical prayers

---

73. Gorman, "John's Implicit Ethic of Enemy-Love," 154.
74. Beutler, *A Commentary on the Gospel of John*, 438.
75. Kanagaraj, "The Implied Ethics of the Fourth Gospel," 61.

that are congruent with the intent of the Law, namely love for God and for others within the community. While the Evangelist does not explicitly prescribe love for those outside the family of God, the textual evidence demonstrates that this is the inevitable trajectory of the FD and the implicit sentiment of prayer in Jesus' name.

Chapter 3

Ethical Prayer in 1 John

IN THE PREVIOUS CHAPTER I explored the relationship between Jesus' love-ethic and petitionary prayer in the FD. In this chapter I will explore select passages in 1 John (3:21–22; 5:14–16) for the purpose of discerning the relationship between these topics in this document. As will be seen in this chapter, both the FD and 1 John highlight the assurance one can have in prayer. Yet, whereas John 14:1, 12–14; and 15:1–7 place belief in Jesus, the efficacy of his name, and abiding in him as the grounds of one's assurance in prayer, I will demonstrate that 1 John embeds the topic of prayer in real-life, ethical scenarios that illustrate how such existential confidence in prayer is achieved and maintained. Moreover, I will show how prayer according to God's will results in confidence before him and has the potential to contribute to the restoration of brothers and sisters who have violated God's ethical standards.

Filling in What the Farewell Discourse Left Out

Much time and space has been devoted to discussing the nature of the Johannine documents, the history of their composition, their authorship,[1] and their backgrounds.[2] More recently, Urban von Wahlde, Paul Anderson, Alan Culpepper, Jan van der Watt, Judith Lieu, and others have moved the scholarly discussion forward by analyzing the situation, composition, and theological content of the Johannine epistles.[3] The fruit of their labor sharpens our understanding of how to interpret the epistles on their own terms and supplements our understanding of their relationship to the FG. In an essay entitled, "Raymond Brown's View of the Crisis of 1 John : In Light of Some Peculiar Features of the Johannine Gospel," Urban Von Wahlde summarizes and interacts with Brown's understanding of the relationship between 1 John and the Johannine tradition of the FG.[4] He agrees with Brown that 1 John was written to correct a misinterpretation of the Gospel's tradition and that "many of the views of the author of 1 John can be found in the Gospel, but that in the Gospel, they represent views that are only minimally present."[5] While space does not permit a complete survey of his analysis, I find his conclusion concerning the relationship between these Johannine documents as plausibly convincing, particularly as it relates to the author of 1 John qualifying and nuancing theological elements that are contained in the Johannine tradition of the FG. As will be discussed in more detail below, without seeking

---

1. While a detailed argument either for or against Johannine authorship is beyond the scope of this chapter, Colin Kruse is right to suggest that if these works were not written by the same author, "then the person(s) who wrote the letters had been deeply immersed in the thought of the Gospel and used its language." Kruse, *The Letters of John*, 2. Therefore, while the FG and 1 John do not necessarily intersect on authorial grounds, the concerns of the community addressed in 1 John are, to some extent, congruent with the interests of the Evangelist in general and with the concerns of the FD where the concepts of belief in Jesus, confidence in prayer, and abiding in truth are elucidated.

2. For a brief overview see Van der Watt, *An Introduction*, 22–25.

3. Culpepper and Anderson, *Communities in Dispute*.

4. Von Wahlde writes, "The 'tract' (Brown's term for 1 John) was intended to put forward the correct interpretation of the Gospel by emphasizing elements that were less dominant, over against what the author thought was a misrepresentation, which focused on elements of the tradition that were dominant in the Gospel." Von Wahlde, "Raymond Brown's View," 23–24.

5. Von Wahlde, "Raymond Brown's View," 25.

to improve on the theological grounds for prayer as they are presented in the FD (Jesus' departure to the Father and the efficacy of his name and indwelling words), the author of 1 John does seek to provide the existential grounds for confidence in prayer and does so in light of the love commandment. The analysis that follows will explore this possibility in more detail.

The Love-Ethic of 1 John

One will search in vain within the Johannine literature for an exhaustive list of ethical behaviors that believers are commanded to live by.[6] For the author of 1 John in particular, ethical outcomes find their basis in the work of the Spirit and the love commandment. And while the FG employs the phrase "born again" (3:3, 7) to describe the work of the Spirit in the new birth, 1 John uniquely describes the corollaries of being "born of God" (e.g., 1 John 3:9-10; 5:1-2) in externalized examples that complement those seen in the FD.[7] As seen in ancient culture, one's birth has implications in their social status and identity. Individuals did not live in autonomy, but in relationship to their Father and their social group. If the "seed" of God (1 John 3:9) abides in the child of God, that individual will act in a manner that honors his Father and the family.[8] Since "God is love" (4:16), the hallmark proofs that one has been "born of God" is his or her "love" for "one another" (4:7). As seen in 3:11-24, the author's train of thought concerning the logical basis for love, its application in the community, and its relationship to prayer is seen in the following summary:

6. Van der Watt remarks, "Ethical behavior involves an obedient relational orientation towards Jesus and the Father and not an adherence to a list of 'do's' and 'do not's.'" Van der Watt, "Mimesis or Imitation," 219.

7. Of course, the FD emphasizes the topic of "love" in numerous contexts, yet it does so without any mention of the new birth. Most specifically "love" is depicted in relationship to the expression it takes in Jesus' love for his disciples (e.g., 13:1-15, 34; 15:12-13; 17:26). Such love, then, is to be externalized through the believing community to replicate Jesus' character and to confirm one's status as an authentic disciple (13:35).

8. See Van der Watt, "Mimesis or Imitation," 205-6.

1. Children in the family of God should love one another. (3:11)
2. Everyone who hates a fellow family member (their "brother") abides in death. (3:14)
3. Jesus modeled what love looks like. (3:16)
4. Believers are to model Jesus' example. (3:16)
5. Failure to meet someone's worldly needs is the antithesis of love. (3:12, 14–15, 17)
6. Laying one's life down is a vital aspect of keeping the commandments of God. (3:16, 23b)
7. This results in having an assured heart before God. (3:19)
8. A heart that is not condemned results in confidence before God. (3:21)
9. Confidence before God results in the privilege of being able to ask for whatever one wishes in prayer and receiving it. (3:22)
10. Obedience to God is evidence that one abides in God. (3:24)
11. We know that we abide in him by the Spirit whom he has given us. (3:24)[9]

In 3:12 the author sets forth an example concerning the antithesis of love in the case of Cain's murder of Abel. Fratricide occurred because Cain's deeds were "evil" and his brother's deeds were "righteous." The author then presents a paradigm that explicates the implications of "hate" and "love" for the believing community. They should not be surprised (v. 13) that the world hates them because they have passed from death to life (v. 14). And the possession of life inevitably leads to the demonstration of love for their brothers and sisters. Conversely, the one who does not love is said to abide in death (v. 14). Rudolf Schnackenburg says that such individuals abide in the "realm of death" and that "God has not accepted them into his realm of life and salvation."[10] In the author's

---

9. This outline originally appeared in my PhD dissertation (Adams, "Prayer in the Farewell Discourse," 332–33).
10. Schnackenburg, *The Johannine Epistles*, 181.

view, there is no middle ground; one is either in the realm of life or the realm of death. At the conceptual level, the author's concept of abiding is congruent (in consequence) with what is seen in the FD, specifically in John 15:2 ("Every branch in me that does not bear fruit he takes away") and 15:6 ("If anyone does not abide in me he is thrown away like a branch and withers; and the branches are gathered, thrown into the fire, and burned"). In the language of the FD, it is said that one may appear to be "in" Jesus, the vine, but failure to bear fruit demonstrates just the opposite. As noted above, abiding in Jesus leads to bearing fruit for Jesus, which inevitably involves the fruit of love. Additionally, the FD and 1 John present the following constructions with the themes of keeping his commandments and the corollaries thereof:

> If you keep my commandments, you will abide in my love. (John 15:10)
>
> Whoever keeps his commandments abides in God, and God in him. (1 John 3:24)

In addition to the *ean* clause in 15:10, the primary difference is seen in the phrases "abides in my love" and "abides in God, and God in him." Notwithstanding, to abide in one is to necessarily abide in the other. Both documents view keeping Jesus' commandment(s) as the proof of abiding. Specifically, obedience not only involves believing in his name, but it also involves loving one another (1 John 3:23). The nature of love is described in 3:16, where the author highlights Jesus' example of laying down his life. But verse 17 provides a negative scenario in which love for one's brother is called into question, "But if anyone has the world's goods and sees his brother in need, yet closes his heart against him, how does God's love abide in him?"[11] In verse 18 the author encourages his audience to love not in word or talk, but "in deed and in truth." Of course, showing love in this manner precludes the validity of a Docetic worldview whereby one could bypass someone with material needs. As Van der Watt remarks, "There was

---

11. Kruse cites Deut 15:7–9 as a possible background to the idea of closing one's heart to others in need. Kruse, *The Letters of John*, 138.

no need for expressing love in physical terms, since only spiritual things count (1 John 3.11–18)."[12] Schnackenburg is right to point out that, although the Docetists whom Ignatius of Antioch battled "cannot be placed on par with the false teachers of 1 John and their Christology, there are nevertheless striking points of similarity."[13] The clearest connection is that both groups not only failed to take Jesus' humanity seriously but they also cared little about the practical, physical needs within the community.[14] Therefore, it is of utmost importance for the brothers and sisters to love according to the tradition of "truth" that was historically defined by the Jesus tradition and transmitted to the believing community.

But how can one know that he is walking in truth? The clause that begins 3:19, namely, "By this we shall know that we are of the truth and reassure our heart before him" connects the preceding statement (3:11–18) to what follows, but it does so in an explanatory sense. One can "know" he is "of the truth" and possess a reassured heart before God by laying down his life for others (as Jesus did).[15] The question of one's knowledge hearkens to 2:3 where the author writes concerning how we can "know" that we "know him," namely, "if we keep his commandments" (2:3). On the other hand, he notes, "Whoever says 'I know him' but does not keep his commandments is a liar, and the truth is not in him" (2:4). As such, epistemic confidence is achieved as one walks in the way Jesus walked (2:6). The one who imitates Jesus may have confidence that he knows him, abides in the sphere of the truth, and is not a liar. Or as I. Howard Marshall states, "Doing what is characteristic of the realm of truth is the sign that we belong to that realm."[16] As will

12. Van der Watt, *An Introduction*, 21.

13. Schnackenburg, *The Johannine Epistles*, 21–22.

14. For a more thorough discussion, see Schnackenburg, *The Johannine Epistles*, 21–23.

15. I. Howard Marshall rightly notes that the author is not referring to our "continual assurance that we belong to God, but rather of the coming of a crisis of belief when we want to know if we belong to God. In such a situation we are to examine ourselves to see whether we are keeping the command given to us by God." Marshall, *The Epistles of John*, 197.

16. Marshall, *The Epistles of John*, 196–97.

be seen below, abiding in the sphere of love and truth has direct implication for prayer.

Confidence in Prayer

The statement in 3:19, "By this we shall know that we are of the truth and reassure our heart before him" is issued for those who, for various reasons, are facing existential uncertainty, an issue that is not addressed in the FD. Perhaps some have overlooked the material needs of others. Perhaps some have realized that they have not loved as Jesus loved. If so, the manner by which one achieves a quieted heart and confidence before God involves laying down one's life for the brothers and sisters. If condemnation persists, one must know that God is greater than their heart.[17] Accordingly, the consequence of having a reassured heart that is not condemned is outlined in the following prerequisite/privilege paradigm in 3:21:

- Prerequisite: "Beloved, if our heart does not condemn us . . ."
- Privilege: ". . . we have confidence [*parrēsia*] before God."

As seen in 3:22:

- Privilege: "and whatever we ask we receive from him, . . ."
- Prerequisite: ". . . because we keep his commandments and do what pleases him."

Verse 21 begins with the vocative (*Agapētoi*) followed by a third-class conditional clause with *ean* introducing the hypothetical scenario, "if our heart does not condemn us . . ." If this condition is fulfilled, then the result is confidence before God. The term *parrēsia* is used in numerous contexts in ancient literature. For example, Philo says that "Joseph, without being at all dismayed at

---

17. Marshall explains, "God's knowledge of all things includes knowledge of us, which is better than our knowledge of ourselves. But the point is not that God is merciful and forgiving (which, of course, John assumes) but that he has full knowledge on which to base a just verdict concerning us." Marshall, *The Epistles of John*, 198n7.

the rank and majesty of the speaker, conversed with him rather as a king with a subject than like a subject with a king, using freedom of speech [*parrēsia*], though mingled with respect."[18] The Testament of Reuben remarks, "For until my father's death I had not boldness [*parrēsia*] to look in his face, or to speak to any of my brethren, because of the reproach. Even until now my conscience causeth me anguish on account of my impiety."[19] In addition to *parrēsia* appearing in numerous contexts throughout the FG, the author of 1 John employs it in the context of Jesus' coming (2:28) and day of judgment (4:17) as well as in prayer (3:21–22; 5:14). In the present context of 3:21, *parrēsia* relates to one's inner condition and outward posture toward God in prayer in the absence of a condemned heart. Such confidence places one before God with a heightened sense of freedom, courage, and expectation.[20]

The author's concept of confidence before God in prayer is congruent with the nature of prayer as it is prescribed in John 14:13–14 and 15:7, 16. In the former case and in 15:16, the condition to having one's prayer answered involves simply making requests in Jesus' name. In 14:13 the phrase *ho ti an*, best translated as "whatever," "anyhow," is followed by the verb *aitēsēte*, thus translated as: "whatever, anyhow you ask." Of course, the request itself has to be congruent with the phrase, *en tō onomati mou*. In the case of 15:7, the condition to having one's prayer answered involves abiding in Jesus and allowing his words to abide within. If the conditions are met, believers may ask whatever they wish and thus have confidence that their prayers will be heard and responded to. While such confidence is implied in 14:13–14 and 15:7, it is explicitly stated in 1 John 3:21–22 by the author's usage of *parrēsia*. The FD and 1 John employ slightly different vocabulary but portray the same optimistic outcomes insofar as prayer is concerned.

---

18. Philo, "On Joseph," in *The Works of Philo*, 444.
19. Charles, *The Testaments of the Twelve Patriarchs*, 9.
20. David Peterson points out that God's love in Christ's atoning death is the ultimate foundation for one's assurance on the day of judgement. But Jesus' love replicated through believers provides practical confidence in prayer. Peterson, "Prayer in the General Epistles," 117.

Furthermore, in the FD faith in Jesus is the remedy for the disciples' troubled hearts, the prerequisite for prayer in his name, the impetus for performance of greater works for the Father's glory. In contrast to the FD, 1 John 3:22 contains no mention of praying in Jesus' name or on the basis of his words (e.g., John 14:13–14; 15:7). There is simply no reason to repeat these elements of prayer. Instead, the author presents "keeping his commandments" and "doing what pleases him" as the necessary conditions for receiving whatever one asks in prayer. However, it is important to note that the *hoti* clause of 1 John 3:22b does not equate God's willingness to hear one's prayers with legalistic obedience to Jesus' commandments.[21] John Stott says, "Obedience is the indispensable condition, not the meritorious cause, of answered prayer."[22] To state it another way, obedience to Jesus flows forth from one's union with Jesus. Strictly speaking, the prerequisite to answered prayer, then, is founded upon a faithful relationship with Jesus; and the one who abides in Jesus will obey him and will be heard by him.

The nature of keeping his commandments is enunciated in 1 John 3:23, namely, "And this is his commandment, that we believe in the name of his Son Jesus Christ and love one another, just as he has commanded us." This commandment and its corollary are stated in slightly different terms in John 15:12–13, namely, "This is my commandment, that you love one another as I have loved you. Greater love has no one than this, that someone lay down his life for his friends." While the nature of Jesus laying down his life is implied in 15:13, the nature of how this applies to believers is explicitly stated in 1 John 3:17: "But if anyone has the world's goods

---

21. See Schnackenburg, *The Johannine Epistles*, 188.
22. Stott, *The Epistles of John*, 149.

and sees his brother in need."[23] Put simply, a person who helps others will be heard by God and will have his prayers answered.[24]

In summary, the author of 1 John expands various themes within the FD in general and its prayer tradition in particular. By doing so, he provides us with a fuller, communally nuanced profile of Johannine prayer that grounds existential confidence in prayer to ethical behaviors performed in the community. Such behaviors do not earn the right to be heard in prayer, but rather serve as indicators that one truly abides in Jesus, knows him, and keeps his commandments.

Praying for the Straying

In 5:14–17, the author of 1 John reiterates the efficacy of prayer, but does so in an ethical context that has more to do with the preservation of the believing community than its numerical growth. In verse 14 the author presents a prerequisite/privilege paradigm.

- Prerequisite: "that if we ask anything according to his will..."
- Privilege: "... he hears us."
- Privilege: "And this is the confidence that we have toward him."

The author continues in 5:15:

- Prerequisite: "And if we know that he hears us in whatever we ask..."
- Privilege: "... we know that we have the requests that we have asked of him."

---

23. Van der Watt writes, "Through his cross, Jesus mediated eternal life for us; through our deeds of compassion and help for those in need, we create life for them. The basic requirement is clear: a follower of Jesus ought to better the lives of brothers in need in practical ways even if it might require sacrifice from the followers of Jesus, perhaps even to the point of laying down one's life." Van der Watt, "Mimesis or Imitation," 218.

24. The preceding three paragraphs originally appeared in my PhD dissertation (Adams, "Prayer in the Farewell Discourse," 335).

The conditional tone of verse 14 is seen in the clause, "if we ask anything according to his will."[25] When the condition is fulfilled, the consequence follows. In this understanding, then, the one who is in a relationship with Jesus will shape his prayers according to the will of Jesus. This is stated clearly in 1 John 5:14, but it is also modeled in the FD where one's asking presupposes belief in Jesus (John 14:1, 12), union with Jesus (15:1–5), and prayer according to the name and words of Jesus (14:13–14; 15:7, 16; 16:23). By stating that the believer must ask in accordance with God's will (1 John 5:14), the author may be collapsing John 14:13–14 (on the basis of Jesus' name) and 15:7 (on the basis of Jesus' words) into one conceptual theme, and, much like 1 John 3:21, he includes the manner by which one may approach God, namely, in confidence. But in contrast to statements in chapters 14 and 15 of John, the author of 1 John explicitly assures his reader in 5:14–15 that they can have confidence in knowing that by asking in accordance with God's will, he will hear their prayer and answer accordingly (v. 15).[26] The author does not speak of the timing of the fulfillment of the request, but he simply notes that the prayer will be heard and attended to.[27]

The author then takes the theme of prayer beyond previous discussions (in both 1 John and the FD) and applies it to another real-life, ethical scenario within the community. He writes in 5:16, "If anyone sees his brother committing a sin not leading to death, he shall ask, and God will give him life." Throughout 1 John the author issues numerous statements about sin (e.g., 1:8–10; 3:4, 8–10). In the present case, the author highlights a brother[28] committing a

25. Brooke Foss Westcott views God's *thelēma* as "the spiritual consummation of man and all external things only so far as they are contributory to this." Westcott, *The Epistles of St. John*, 190.

26. John Painter correctly says, "The conclusion of 5:14, 'he hears us,' now becomes the basis of the condition of 5:15." Painter, *1, 2, and 3 John*, 314.

27. The content of this paragraph originally appeared in my PhD dissertation (Adams, "Prayer in the Farewell Discourse," 336).

28. Marshall sees "brother" as another church member. Marshall, *The Epistles of John*, 246. Westcott notes, "The sight of sin in 'a brother'—a fellow Christian—and it is only with Christians that St John is dealing—necessarily stirs to intercession." Westcott, *The Epistles of St. John*, 191.

sin, but the exact details of this sin are not specified except that it does not lead to death. While it is impossible to be sure, perhaps he is thinking about a brother who has strayed from the commandment of love by overlooking someone's material needs. In this reading, this sort of sinning has ethical implications. And the one who fails to love abides in death and has no assurance before God in prayer. Conversely, the one who abides in Jesus and obeys his commandments has confidence in prayer and may in fact be the one who, by his prayers, is instrumental in bringing a sinner back to life.[29] Of course, a true brother already possesses life (3:14; 5:11, 12, 13), which indicates reception of and adherence to the truth. Yet by virtue of a transgression that is not injurious or hopelessly antithetical to his profession of faith, he may require restoration. Life, as it were, is not intrinsically lost to the sinner, but his existential awareness and joy of it may be disrupted.[30] The author connects life to fellowship with God (1:1–4) but notes that such fellowship is interrupted when someone walks in darkness (1:6). Nevertheless, here he places responsibility on the one who sees a brother sinning to participate in his restoration through prayer. As far as John 15:7–8 is concerned, answered prayer is the corollary of a faithful relationship with Jesus and is the means by which "much fruit" (disciples) is produced. In the context of 1 John 5:16, prayer offered by the faithful community functions as the means by which sinning disciples are restored and preserved. The author does not provide a precise formula for the one praying but simply highlights the consequence of his prayers.[31]

---

29. Kruse cites three possible ways to view this statement. He states, "In answer to prayer (a) God will give repentant believers reconfirmation of their transfer from the realm of death to the realm of life; (b) God will grant forgiveness to the repentant believer, and receiving forgiveness means having life with God; (c) God will give the promised resurrection life to sinning believers who repent." Kruse, *The Letters of John*, 191.

30. Westcott agrees and states further, "Life is fellowship with Christ. Death is separation from Him. All sin tends to make fellowship less complete. Yet not all equally; nor all fixed and unalterable degrees." Westcott, *The Epistles of St. John*, 191.

31. The content of this paragraph originally appeared in my PhD dissertation (Adams, "Prayer in the Farewell Discourse," 309).

Finally, the author says that there is a certain sin that "leads to death" (5:16). In this case, he says, "I do not say that one should pray for that" (*ou peri ekeinēs legō hina erōtēsē*). Does the author's usage of *erōtaō* instead of *aiteō* indicate that one should not ask a question about the nature of the sin? As is widely known, *erōtaō* can mean either to "ask a question" (e.g., John 16:5, 23) or to "request" something in prayer (e.g., 17:9, 20). While it is hard to be certain, Ramey Michaels following Paul Trudinger, is probably right in saying that the former understanding is what the author had in mind. He says, "Believers should go ahead and pray for a sinning brother or sister without raising the question whether or not the sin is 'mortal' or 'leads to death.'"[32] If the latter meaning is utilized then the author discourages (but does not necessarily forbid) making requests for the one sinning unto death.

While a thorough analysis of a sin unto death is beyond the scope of the present discussion, there are instances in the Old Testament and in other Jewish literature where it is said that sin led to people's physical demise (e.g., Num 18:22; Deut 22:25–26; Isa 22:14).[33] Likewise, the New Testament reports instances where it is said that certain individuals died physically because of sin (Acts 5:1–11; most likely in 1 Cor 5:3–5). The most serious sins(s) in 1 John involve rejection of the truth and unwillingness to walk in the truth. Such people are described as "antichrists" (1 John 2:18), those who deny that Jesus is the Christ (2:22), and those who seek to deceive (2:26). Their ongoing unbelief and rejection of Jesus may be properly labeled a sin "that leads to death." Such sin is displayed by the Pharisees whom Jesus chastises (John 9:40–41). In this case, those who claim to see are blind. And such blindness pertains not only to one's self-awareness of sin but also to the truth concerning the person and work of Christ. In light of John 16:9, it is evident that the Spirit will convict the world in regard to sin because people

---

32. Michaels, "Finding Yourself an Intercessor," 247.

33. Marshall helpfully points out the distinction in the OT between two types of sin: intentional and unintentional. The latter could be atoned for through animal sacrifice, whereas the former was dealt with through physical death. Marshall, *The Epistles of John*, 246.

do not believe. If this verse is applied to the community that 1 John addresses, then it is not the absence of conviction that brings condemnation but rather a willful disregard for the truth that has been elucidated. In the end, those who refuse to believe are said to "die in their sin" (John 8:21). While physical death may be in view, the more probable explanation is that, by virtue of their rejection of Christ, the sinning party spoken of by the author of 1 John is in a state that will lead to his spiritual demise.[34] Moreover, from the vantage point of 1 John 5:14–16, believers who pray according to God's will work in tandem with God to preserve "brothers" in the community who are also not of this world. By praying for a brother (whose sin does not lead to death), believers in the community mimic Jesus' prayer in John 17 wherein he requests that believers will be kept, protected, and unified (vv. 12, 14, 17, 21, and 23).[35]

Conclusion

In this chapter I have argued that it is possible that the author of 1 John was not satisfied with the prayer tradition of the FD and therefore sought to provide an expanded, nuanced account concerning the conditions and outcomes of prayer. Notwithstanding, both documents highlight the assurance one can have in prayer—whether one prays for the numerical growth of the community or

34. John Painter sees the sin unto death as related to the author's opponents who "rejected the confession that Jesus Christ has come in the flesh and the obligation of love that flowed from it." Painter, *1, 2, and 3 John*, 317. Marshall concurs but says further, "It is evident that the author is most concerned about the sins which are most incompatible with being a child of God, and these are summed up in the denial that Jesus is the Son of God, refusal to obey God's command, love of the world, and hatred of one's brother. Such sins are characteristic of the person who belongs to the sphere of darkness rather than the sphere of light." Marshall, *The Epistles of John*, 246–47. Kruse states accordingly, "They are people who deny that Jesus is the Christ come in the flesh, and also deny the significance of his atoning death. This would mean that they place themselves outside the sphere of forgiveness, and their sins become the sin unto death." Kruse, *The Letters of John*, 192.

35. The bulk of this paragraph originally appeared in my PhD dissertation (Adams, "Prayer in the Farewell Discourse," 311–12).

its ethical and confessional fidelity—and they do so in a complementary, but nuanced manner. Whereas John 14:1, 12–14; and 15:1–7 place belief in Jesus, the efficacy of his name, and abiding in him as the grounds of one's assurance in prayer, 1 John embeds the topic of prayer in real-life, ethical scenarios that illustrate how such existential confidence in prayer is achieved. Obedience is not the ground of one's confidence in prayer, but is rather the fruit of one's union with Jesus that is made possible by his atoning sacrifice. But the one who abides in the sphere of love will bear the fruit of love as he imitates Jesus' character. While confidence in prayer is implied in John 14:13–14 and 15:7, it is explicitly stated in 1 John 3:21–22 by the author's usage of *parrēsia*. Hence, the FD and 1 John employ slightly different vocabulary but portray the same optimistic outcomes insofar as prayer is concerned. As far as 1 John is concerned, one can pray confidently for a brother or sister who is committing a sin that does not lead to death. While the nature of such sinning is not specified, the author of 1 John clearly indicates that the believer's prayer is the means by which a brother or sister is restored to life.

Chapter 4

Missional Prayer in 3 John

IN THE PREVIOUS CHAPTER I examined prayer passages in the FD and 1 John. In this chapter I will seek to determine the function of prayer in 3 John 2 with respect to the term *euchomai*. While this word can mean either "wish" or "pray," I will argue that the author utilizes it to indicate his desire for Gaius's overall well-being and as a petition to God for this desire to come to pass as Gaius supports the mission of God. Accordingly, this chapter will examine prayer in 3 John on its own terms, but it will also seek to discover how the Elder's prayer-wish compares to prayer in the FD. In particular, attention will be given to discerning the relationship between prayer, the fruitfulness of believers, and the mission of God in 3 John and the FD.

Overview of 3 John

Third John is the shortest document in the New Testament and stands as the only book within it that does not mention Jesus or Christ. The author of 3 John begins by identifying himself as "the elder" and offers a warm, affectionate address to "the beloved Gaius" (also the vocative, *Agapēte* in vv. 2, 5, 11). Gaius was a common name, appearing several places in the New Testament (Acts 19:29; 20:4; Rom 16:23; 1 Cor 1:14). However, it is unlikely that any of these individuals are the Gaius whom the Elder addresses in 3 John

Missional Prayer in 3 John

1. Besides what is briefly written in this epistle, we know nothing else of the Gaius of 3 John. Yet, based on the Elder's remarks, it is clear enough that he and Gaius enjoyed "close and warm ties."[1] Notwithstanding, verse 3 indicates that certain brothers brought a report that testified to Gaius's "truth" which brought great joy to the Elder (v. 4). The Elder is not merely thinking of theological or doctrinal truth, but the way of truth expressed in Gaius showing hospitality to the travelers who found refuge in his home.[2] As noted in verses 5–7, certain brothers/strangers who "have gone out for the sake of the name" (v. 7), were to be refreshed and sent on their way (v. 6), well-resourced for their journey.[3] Verse 6 indicates that these emissaries testified concerning Gaius's love before the church. Alan Culpepper is right in saying, "He [Gaius] had simply distinguished himself by his willingness to provide hospitality for fellow Christians. Hospitality was a sign of love (v. 6), which confirmed that Gaius lived in the truth (v. 3)."[4]

Furthermore, the Johannine community experienced a degree of conflict and turmoil, which necessitated a response from the Elder, who sent a letter, followed by the emissaries. Both were rejected by Diotrephes (3 John 9–10).[5] The complaints against him are enumerated in verses 9–10: (1) he likes to put himself first, (2) he does not acknowledge appointed authority, (3) he talks wicked

---

1. See Yarbrough, *1–3 John*, 365.

2. For a brief description and overview of the place and time of the early Christian gatherings, see Cullmann, *Early Christian Worship*, 9–12.

3. Judith Lieu notes, "The narrative of 3 John is episodic rather than linear, and the writing of the letter is only indirectly and partially effective within it, namely, to provoke Gaius into continuing his current activity." Lieu, "The Audience of the Johannine Epistles," 133.

4. See Culpepper, *The Gospel and Letters of John*, 280.

5. Von Wahlde summarizes circumstances of the community by writing, "The author, in his letter to Gaius, refers to reports he has received from travelers coming from Gaius's community. The Elder also speaks of another group of travelers who had come to the community where Diotrephes was a member. This second group of travelers seems to have come from the community of the Elder with a letter of recommendation written by the Elder. But Diotrephes did not accept the recommendation and so rejected the travelers [3 John 9–10]." Von Wahlde, *The Gospel and Letters of John*, 248–49.

nonsense against the Elder and his associates, (4) he refuses to welcome the brothers, and (5) he prevents others who want to and puts them out of the church.[6] The Elder's strategy for dealing with Diotrephes is stated in verse 10, "So if I come, I will bring up what he is doing, talking wicked nonsense against us." Schnackenburg sees this statement as implying a "serious public rebuke" rather than "disciplinary action."[7] Finally, after commending Demetrius (v. 12) as one who received a good testimony from everyone, the Elder concludes by expressing his desire to see Gaius soon (v. 14), and by offering a greeting (v. 15).

Pray or Wish?

In a manner that accords with a standard health wish of the ancient world,[8] the Elder says in verse 2, "Beloved, I pray [*euchomai*] that all may go well with you and that you may be in good health, as it goes well with your soul."[9] The Elder's choice of wording is curious. The term *euchomai* can have the force of "to pray" (Acts 26:29; 2 Cor 13:7, 9; Jas 5:16) or "to wish" (Rom 9:3). As one reviews the scholarly literature, many commentators insist the Elder is simply offering his "wish" that Gaius would prosper and experience good health.[10] Thus Brown remarks, "The use of the verb in

---

6. Numerous suggestions have been put forth concerning the nature of the power struggle between the Elder and Diotrephes. Some have suggested that it was theological in nature, while others suggest that it was personal. For an overview of these views, see Malherbe, *Social Aspects of Early Christianity*, 93-94.

7. Schnackenburg, *The Johannine Epistles*, 297.

8. Robert Funk remarks, "The conventional health wish in III John 2 marks this letter as the most secularized in the NT." He goes on to admit that the structure of 3 John seems to "exhibits more affinities with the Pauline—and thus the Christian—letter format than does II John" and thus corresponds to the "Pauline order." Funk, "The Form and Structure of II and III John," 430.

9. D. Moody Smith sees 3 John 2-3 as containing "the rudiments of an opening prayer or thanksgiving, similar to the Pauline thanksgiving (e.g., 1 Cor. 4-9) that were more or less conventional in ancient Hellenistic letters." Smith, *First, Second, and Third John*, 150.

10. See Funk, "The Form and Structure of II and III John," 424-25.

secular letters as a polite wish for health means that receivers of a New Testament letter would interpret it the same way unless there was a contextual indication of a more profound intent, and that is lacking here."[11] If nothing further was intended, the Elder's wish for Gaius's well-being accords with the affectionate tone that is expressed toward him throughout the letter (vv. 1, 3, 5, 11). However, while a wish of well-being elucidates the nature of the Elder's posture toward Gaius, the wish does not, on its own, have the causal power to bring forth the desired result. It is merely a conventional wish. But a wish communicated to God in the form of prayer becomes petitionary and potentially effectual. Therefore, Stephen Smalley is right to say, "In view of the content of 3 John as a whole, the verb probably heralds the beginning of an actual prayer. The presbyter's missive is not entirely 'secular.'"[12] It is also possible that 3 John 2 provides an instance of *double entendre* where both "wish" and "pray" are intended.[13] In this reading the Elder may have employed *euchomai* to accomplish two tasks at once: (1) to convey his gracious wishful desire for Gaius's overall well-being, and (2)

Schnackenburg says, "The good wishes usual in ancient letters for the welfare and health of the recipients are employed here by the Christian author....The elder wishes for Gaius the spiritual well-being that he also wishes for him physically." Schnackenburg, *The Johannine Epistles*, 292. Accordingly, Von Wahlde writes, "This word is related to the verb for prayer (*proseuchomai*) but does not necessarily imply that the wish is directed to God. The more conventional meaning 'I wish' is also possible." Von Wahlde, *The Gospel and Letters of John*, 255. Jobes remarks, "Because the verb 'I pray' (εὔχομαί) is part of the conventional phrase, it should not be pressed for a more specific Christian or theological reading.... Given the idiomatic nature of the expression, prayer should not be the main exegetical point of the passage." Jobes, *1, 2, & 3 John*, 290. Bultmann says that *euchomai* and its preceding terms "hardly refers to prayer, but is simply a wish in conformity with typical epistolary style." Bultmann, *The Johannine Epistles*, 97n1. Finally, Georg Strecker agrees by saying, "One should not here think of a prayer for the sick (as in Js 5:15), and it is questionable whether the idea of petitionary prayer is implied, for in that case one would expect the dative construction ('to God')." Strecker, *The Johannine Letters*, 256n6.

11. Brown, *The Epistles of John*, 703.
12. See Smalley, *1, 2, 3 John*, 345.
13. See Kruse, *The Letters of John*, 221; Akin, *1, 2, 3 John*, 240.

to offer a genuine petition to God for this wish to come to pass.[14] Accordingly, in James 5:15–16, the author uses *euchē* (noun) and *euchesthe* (verb) in the context of effectual petitionary prayer.

> And the prayer [*euchē*] of faith will save the one who is sick, and the Lord will raise him up. And if he has committed sins, he will be forgiven. Therefore, confess your sins to one another and pray [*euchesthe*] for one another, that you may be healed. The prayer of a righteous person has great power as it is working.

In 2 Corinthians 13:7, Paul employs this term in a petitionary context that the Corinthians will do no wrong.

> But we pray [*euchometha*] to God that you may not do wrong—not that we may appear to have met the test, but that you may do what is right, though we may seem to have failed.

Further, consider the following letter from the second century wherein a prayer to the gods is offered and a favorable response from the gods is anticipated.

> Apollinarius to Taesis, his mother and lady, many greetings. Before all I pray that you are well, as I myself am well and make supplication for you to the gods here. I want you to know, mother, that I arrived in Rome on the 25th of the month Pachon and was posted to Misenum, although I did not yet know my company. For I had not reached Misenum when I wrote you this letter. I ask you, therefore, mother, take care of yourself and do not worry about me; for I have come to a good position. Please write me a letter concerning your welfare and that of my brothers and all your people. And whenever I find someone I shall write to you; I shall not delay writing. I greet my brethren at length and Apollinarius and his children and Karalas and his children. I greet Ptolemaeus and her

---

14. See also Gary Derickson's discussion of the range of interpretative approaches. Derickson, *First, Second, and Third John*, 661.

MISSIONAL PRAYER IN 3 JOHN

children Heraclous and her children. I greet all who love you by name. I pray for your health.[15]

If one reads 3 John 2 as a prayer, what is the Elder praying for in particular? Von Wahlde notes the chiastic structure of this verse that has often gone unnoticed.

> Beloved, I pray that,
> +in all things,
> +you are doing well
> and
> +that you are in good health
> +just as ( ) is doing well
> +(your soul).[16]

In this arrangement, the first element parallels "in all things" (*peri pantōn*) with "your soul" in the last element (*euodoutai sou hē pyschē*). The second and second-last clauses center on "doing well" and being in "good health." Von Wahlde remarks further, "Thus, together the first and second elements constitute the general wish that Gaius do well 'in all things,' and the last two elements provide a point of comparison by means of a reference to the fact that Gaius is "doing well" spiritually."[17] Accordingly, the Elder views Gaius's spiritual health as the standard for his desire that Gaius experience well-being in all things. R. C. H Lenski says that the Elder's "prayer is that the earthly prosperity of Gaius may be equal to his spiritual prosperity. John makes the well-being of the soul the governing concern; the material is to be 'even as' (*kathōs*) the spiritual. The two cannot be reversed."[18] Throughout the Johannine literature the term *pyschē* refers to the physical life of a person. For example, Jesus says in John 10:11, "I am the good shepherd. The good shepherd lays down his life [*psychēn*] for the sheep." In John 13:37, Peter boldly declares to Jesus, "I will lay down my life [*psychēn*] for you." Finally, in 1 John 3:16 the author says, "By this we know

---

15. As quoted by Lieu *I, II, & III John*, 265.
16. See Von Wahlde, *The Gospel and Letters of John*, 253, 270.
17. Von Wahlde, *The Gospel and Letters of John*, 270.
18. Lenski, *Interpretation*, 578.

love, that he laid down his life [*psychēn*] for us, and we ought to lay down our lives [*psychas*] for the brothers." Tom Thatcher says that *psychē* "evokes spiritual connotations, but the Greek word refers more generally to the biological force in living things."[19] In the present context of 3 John 2, this term refers more strictly to Gaius's spiritual life. Thus, the Elder's prayer-wish is for Gaius's physical health to prosper as his soul (spiritual health) prospers along the journey of life.

The Purpose of the Prayer Wish

But what is the purpose of Gaius's prosperity? Again, verses 3–4 emphasizes that Gaius is "walking in the truth," which in turn gives the Elder great joy. In verses 5–6, the Elder emphasizes the faithful thing Gaius has done in his efforts and love, which are most certainly corollaries of his faith and religious commitments. Kruse notes, "The elder seems to be emphasizing here that Gaius's faithfulness involves not only holding to correct doctrine, but also persisting in correct action. In the context of this letter that correct action is thought of primarily in terms of providing hospitality to those itinerant preachers who deserve support."[20] Further, the Elder encourages Gaius to love and care for the "brothers" (who are also *xenous*) in the future in the same way he has in the past and to send them on in a manner worthy of God (v. 6b). These "brothers" are the ones who went out for "the sake of the name" (which likely refers to the name of Jesus, his authority, and all that his name implies)[21] and refused support from "unbelievers" (or "the nations,"

---

19. Thatcher, *3 John*, 530.
20. Kruse, *The Letters of John*, 221.
21. Bultmann says this phrase "can only mean 'for Christ,' i.e., to proclaim him." Bultmann, *The Johannine Epistles*, 99. Lieu notes, "Elsewhere, 'the name' (*to onoma*), usually identified as that of Jesus, is the means of forgiveness (1 John 2:12), the cause of hatred (John 15:21), the source of miracles (Acts 4:30), the object of faith (John 1:12; 1 John 5:13), the means of life (John 20:31), the framework within which requests can be made (John 14:13), and that into which believers are baptized (Acts 2:38; 10:48). In all these settings it represents the person, and carries with in their authority—the early believers

lambanontes apo tōn ethnikōn). It is not clear from the immediate context what sort of support Gaius and the Christian community might provide, but one might imagine that it included everything needed for missionary endeavors, including but not limited to lodging, food, and basic necessities for evangelism, teaching, and other forms of ministry.[22] Missionary support is the basic corollary and expression of Christian love and serves as the means by which Gaius (and the community) became a co-laborer with the emissaries. Such loving hospitality stands in sharp contrast to the inhospitality of Diotrephes. Therefore, on the basis of verses 3–8, it is plausible to suggest that the Elder's prayer-wish was not made for Gaius's benefit alone, but also for the benefit of the emissaries under his care. The emissaries' well-being is inextricably linked to Gaius's well-being. As Gaius prospered spiritually and physically,

---

were defined by being under Jesus' lordship and with access to his power." Lieu, *I, II, & III John*, 271–72.

22. See Von Wahlde, *The Gospel and Letters of John*, 277. Also, for a discussion on the decline of hospitality in pagan world of the first-century (CE), as well as an overview transient nature of early Christians and the hospitality afforded them by their fellow-believers, see Malherbe, *Social Aspects of Early Christianity* (2003). He writes, "The mobility which characterized the period brought with it a system of inns which sought to meet the needs and desires of travelers. The inns, however, did not enjoy a good reputation among the upper classes, being considered centers of all sorts of nefarious activities and offering poor service. Whenever possible, therefore, discriminating travelers availed themselves of the hospitality of business associates and other acquaintances. The early church reflects the mobility of Roman society as well as the practice of private hospitality. The Book of Acts presents Paul as establishing churches on the main trade routes of the empire and having among his first associates and coverts people who were, like himself, transients. Paul's own letters further impress one with the mobility of his co-workers. It is understandable, that, in view of the conditions of the inns, Christian travelers would prefer to avail themselves of the hospitality of their brethren. The Book of Acts shows a social interest in the practice; it is presupposed in Paul's letters as he plans his own as well his co-workers' travels, and it appears frequent in paraenesis. A virtually technical vocabulary developed to describe the hospitable reception (compounds of *lambano* and *dechomai*) and sending on (*propempo*) of those individuals who were spreading the faith." Malherbe, *Social Aspects of Early Christianity*, 95–96.

the emissaries' needs would be met and the mission of God would continue to advance in an inhospitable world.²³

Toward a Johannine Synthesis

While there is no consensus on the matter, many scholars believe that the FG and 3 John were written by the same author.²⁴ If not, it is plausible to suggest that they share a common tradition.²⁵ Notwithstanding, 3 John is drastically different from the FD. Third John is a letter to an individual disciple, not a farewell speech to multiple disciples. Third John utilizes *euchomai* as an introductory prayer-wish; the FD utilizes terms such as *aiteō* (by disciples) and *erōtaō* by Jesus), and does so as a part of a larger theological discussion. Many other examples can be cited. However, one significant similarity does exist: although the terminology differs from document to document, prayer in both the FD and 3 John is offered for the well-being and/or fruitfulness of the Johannine community.²⁶ In their own unique ways, these documents present a close relationship between prayer and the mission of God.²⁷ With

---

23. Lenski writes, "This concern about the earthly prosperity of Gaius in all his affairs about the good health refers to the ability of Gaius to take care of the missionaries whom John is sending from time to time." Lenski, *Interpretation*, 578.

24. For discussions on the authorship of the Johannine Epistles and their relationship with one another, see Schnackenburg, *The Johannine Epistles*, 291; Kruse, *The Letters of John*, 7–13; Van der Watt, *An Introduction*, 20–22; and Lieu, "The Audience of the Johannine Epistles," 126–32.

25. Von Wahlde contends that 3 John was likely produced at some point during the third edition of the FG, although this is debatable. Von Wahlde, *The Gospel and Letters of John*, 247.

26. Of course, chapter 17 does not prescribe how and why disciples are to pray. Instead, this chapter specifically records Jesus' petitions for his disciples in light of his impending departure. It looks backward, but it also looks forward.

27. In contradistinction to Jesus' prayers in John 6:11; 11:41b–42; 12:27–28; and 19:28, 30, prayer in John 14–16 prescribes *how* and *why* prayer is offered in Jesus' physical absence, namely for the fruitfulness of believers as they carry forth the mission of God in the world.

this similarity in mind, the synthesis that follows does not assume literary dependence between these documents but rather seeks to place them in conversation with one another for the purpose of obtaining a fuller understanding of Johannine prayer.

Comparing John 14:12-14 with 3 John

As far as John 14-17 is concerned, the topic of prayer appears within the context of what seems to be an eschatological crisis: Jesus' departure to the Father is at hand (13:36), the disciples' hearts are troubled (14:1), the mission of God is incomplete (16:32), and tribulation is certain (15:18-21; 16:1-4, 33).[28] In its final form, the FD is arranged in a manner that provides solutions to the problems at hand. As disciples remain in relationship with Jesus and pray according to his name and words (14:13-14; 15:7, 16; 16:23-24), they may, in turn, offer effectual prayer to God that results in them performing "greater works" (14:12) and producing "much fruit" for God (15:8). In brief, Johannine problems are solved through a faithful relationship to Jesus, through whom prayer is offered to God.[29] This discussion is set against the backdrop of John 13 wherein Jesus is presented as the loving host who shares a final meal with his disciples. Perhaps most striking about this account is the hospitality Jesus shows through foot-washing (13:5). This act of service demonstrates the depth of Jesus' humility and points to the need for and reality of cleansing through his cross-death. Brown writes,

> Since feet shod only in sandals tend to get dusty on unpaved roads, it was customary hospitality to provide water for a guest to wash his own feet. But as the Midrash

---

28. Brown notes, "The introduction (xiii 31-38) announced the theme of Jesus' departure; what follows in the Last Discourse is concerned with answering the problems raised by this departure—not the problems of what will happen to Jesus (his glorification is only mentioned), but the problems of what will happen to the disciples he leaves behind." Brown, *The Gospel according to John*, 622-23.

29. As noted in Adams, *Prayer in John's Farewell Discourse*, 201-2.

Mekilta on Exod xxi 2 tells us, the washing of a master's feet could not be required of a Jewish slave. As a sign of devotion, however, occasionally disciples would render this service to their teacher or rabbi; and Jesus seems to allude to this custom in vss. 13-14. Thus, in footwashing Jesus humiliates himself and takes on the form of a servant.[30]

Jesus' work of hospitality stands in sharp contrast to the inhospitality of the unbelieving Jews who refused to receive him (John 1:9-11; 5:16-18; 7:1; 10:31, 39; 11:8, 53),[31] but it is indicative of Jesus' love for his disciples. Since Jesus washed his disciples' feet, they "ought to wash one another's feet" (13:14). The theme of loving hospitality finds appropriate application in the life and ministry of Gaius (3 John 1-6), which may have included the provision of food, resources, and other forms of service. Gaius had faithfully cared for "the brothers" (3 John 3-5) in the past, and it was the Elder's prayer-wish that it would continue to go well with Gaius so that he could care for them again in the future (3 John 6). His actions would naturally serve as an indication that he and the community were truly Jesus' disciples (John 13:35). Further, Gaius's desire to put others first stands in sharp contrast to Diotrephes, who put himself first (3 John 9).

In a carefully arranged manner, in John 14 the Evangelist places prayer within the larger discussion of "believing" in Jesus and performing "greater works" than Jesus. The performance of such works finds it basis in Jesus' departure to the Father and requests made in his name.

Jesus says in verse 12,

> Truly, truly, I say to you, whoever believes in me will also do the works that I do; and greater works than these will he do, because I am going to the Father.

30. Brown, *The Gospel according to John*, 564.

31. That "the Jews" are a group of religious authority figures with an antagonistic attitude toward Jesus is indicated throughout the FG. For example, "the Jews" question Jesus and his teaching (John 2:18, 20; 6:52), they want to kill him (5:18; 7:1), they grumble against him (6:41), and they do not believe him (9:18).

Missional Prayer in 3 John

He continues in verses 13-14:

> Whatever you ask in my name, this I will do, that the Father may be glorified in the Son. If you ask me anything in my name, I will do it.

As seen above, prayer is to be offered in Jesus' name, which means making requests in light of all that his name implies. As I have stated elsewhere, "The name of Jesus encapsulates his nature and earthly mission, which involved performing the works of the Father, offering salvation to all who believe, and bringing glory to the Father."[32] In short, prayer in the name of Jesus produces the works of Jesus through believing disciples. And as argued in chapter 2, such works involve the disciples carrying forth the mission of God in Jesus' physical absence. In this reading, one may ask for "anything" that contributes to or advances the cause of Jesus' mission in the world.

This genre of prayer accords with the prayer-wish of 3 John 2, which centers on Gaius's well-being for the sake of the emissaries under his care. In John 14:13-14, the focus centers on prayer in Jesus' name. In 3 John 2 and 7, the focus centers on prayer for those who "have gone out for the sake of the name" (i.e., Jesus). As it goes well with Gaius in all things, he is thus able to support these emissaries who will perform "greater works" among the churches and carry forth the mission of God. In this wholistic reading, Gaius's prosperity and the corollaries thereof are interpreted in light of Johannine categories and their theological contours. On one hand, this reading necessarily rules out attempts to view the Elder's prayer wish as the means for all Christians to obtain health and wealth. On the other hand, one must not entirely minimize the Elder's prayer-wish to the point of precluding any expectation for material blessing. More precisely, according to the Johannine testimony, one's prayer-wish should center on asking for "whatever" or "anything" that accords with Jesus' name and brings glory to the Father (John 14:13-14). In practical terms, this involves the health

---

32. Adams, *Prayer in John's Farewell Discourse*, 88-89.

(both spiritual and physical) and the resources to carry forth the mission of God.

Comparing John 15:7 with 3 John

In John 15:1–6, the Evangelist introduces the theme of the vine (Jesus), the branch(es) (disciple[s]), and the vine-dresser (the Father). In this paradigm, emphasis is placed on remaining faithful to Jesus. The verb *menō* occurs throughout the FG and generally means "to stay," "to remain/abide," or "to dwell" and is used in reference to remaining in a physical place (e.g., John 1:38, 39; 4:40; 7:9; 10:40; 11:6, 54). However, the Evangelist's usage of *menō* in chapters 14–15 is not employed in the context of a physical place[33] in general but in the context of a relational space in particular. The Spirit (1:32–33) and the Father (14:10) remain in Jesus, and the Spirit (14:17) and Jesus (15:4) remain in disciples.[34] Accordingly, in 15:7 the emphasis is placed on disciples remaining/abiding in Jesus, his words remaining in them, and the corollaries thereof. For example,

> If you abide in me, and my words abide in you, ask whatever you wish, and it will be done for you.

The implications are clear, namely, those who remain in relationship with Jesus (the vine) receive the nourishing sap of his words,

---

33. Köstenberger notes, "Initially, 'remaining with Jesus' simply meant for Jesus' first followers to spend the night in Jesus' apartment (1:38–39). But already in 6:56, Jesus uses this term with a strongly spiritual connotation. . . . Thus, 'remaining in Jesus' entails appropriating his sacrifice at the cross and living in existential identification with him." Köstenberger, *Encountering John*, 161.

34. Keener remarks, "Others in the Gospel had already experienced a foretaste of this life by staying or being with him [Jesus] during his ministry (1:38–39; 4:40; 7:33; 11:54; 13:33; 14:17, 25; 16:4). Now through the Spirit the disciples would dwell with him and he with them in a more intimate manner (6:56; 14:17; 15:4-10); in contrast to the religious-political elite (5:38), they themselves would become his dwelling places (14:23); this is the intimacy Jesus shared with the Father (14:10)." Keener, *The Gospel of John*, 999.

MISSIONAL PRAYER IN 3 JOHN

which, in turn, influence the nature of one's prayer-requests to God. Van der Watt notes:

> Whatever the person wants and asks, will be given to him. This does not refer to just any type of will (just as fruit does not refer to merely any action), but to a will corresponding to the words/revelation of Jesus. If the words of Jesus are in you, you will be guided by them. Jesus has a definite influence on the disciples in the sense that their wishes (7c-e) and their actions (fruit) are adapted to and changes according to the will of God.[35]

Faithful disciples will not ask for anything that precludes Jesus' character and mission. Instead, the content of their requests will be formed upon the basis of their union with Jesus and out of loyalty to him. As indicated in 15:7, as disciples pray according to Jesus' words they will receive anything they ask. The results are that they will bear "much fruit" (15:5) and that their "fruit should abide" (15:16). As I have argued elsewhere, "In bearing much fruit, they [the disciples] have the potential to: (1) produce many new disciples who (2) obey Jesus' commandments and therefore (3) replicate his character in acts of love and service to one another (13:34-35)."[36] Although not explicitly stated, the overall context of 3 John suggests that the Elder's prayer-wish centers on Gaius prospering (or, in the terminology of John 15, bearing "much fruit") for the sake of the mission of God.[37] As Gaius prospers, those under his care will prosper. As he bears much fruit, the emissaries will also bear much fruit. They have the potential to: (1) produce many new disciples who (2) obey Jesus' commandments

---

35. Van der Watt, *Family of the King*, 43.

36. Adams, "Prayer in Johannine Perspective," 113.

37. Carson suggests more broadly "that the 'fruit' in the vine imagery represents everything that is the product of effective prayer in Jesus's name, including obedience to Jesus's commands (v. 10), experience of Jesus's joy (v. 11—as earlier his peace, 14:27), love for one another (v. 12), and witness to the world (vv. 16, 27)." He continues, "This fruit is nothing less than the outcome of preserving dependence on the vine, driven by faith, embracing all of the believer's life and the product of his witness." Carson, *The Gospel according to John*, 517, 523.

and therefore (3) replicate his character in acts of love and service to one another. In short, the Elder's prayer-wish for Gaius has the potential to contribute to his spiritual and physical fruitfulness and, by necessity, the emissaries' spiritual and physical fruitfulness. Although the terminology varies, the outcome of prayer in John 15 is conceptually and practically congruent with the prayer-wish of 3 John 2.

Comparing John 17 with 3 John

In John 17 the Evangelist records Jesus' lengthy prayer to the Father. In its final form this prayer precedes his departure across the Kidron Valley (18:1–12).[38] Since the sixteenth century chapter 17 has been recognized as Jesus' "High Priestly Prayer," even though this prayer does not present Jesus in such terms.[39] Perhaps the most appropriate term to describe John 17 is "communion," although only the Son speaks.[40] As Jesus communes with his Father, he offers a report concerning the status of his earthly mission. After asking the Father to glorify the Son so that the Son may glorify the Father (vv. 1, 4–5), Jesus issues several statements that elucidate his obedience to the will of the Father. For example:

> "I glorified you on earth, having accomplished the work that you gave me to do." (v. 4)
> "I have manifested your name to the people whom you gave me out of the world." (v. 6)
>
> "For I have given them the words that you gave me, and they have received them
> and have come to know in truth that I came from you;
> and they have believed that
> you sent me." (v. 8)

---

38. Johannes Beutler says that one can regard chapter 17 as "a continuation of the farewell discourse or a concluding summary." Beutler, *A Commentary on the Gospel of John*, 425.

39. See Carson, *The Gospel according to John*, 552–53.

40. As noted by Stevick, *Jesus and His Own*, 309.

Missional Prayer in 3 John

> "While I was with them, I kept them in your name, which you have given me. I have guarded them, and not one of them has been lost except the son of destruction, that the Scripture might be fulfilled." (v. 12)

> "As you sent me into the world, so I have sent them into the world." (v. 18)

In this prayer-report Jesus indicates that he accomplished the Father's work, manifested the Father's name, spoke the Father's words, and kept and guarded the disciples whom the Father gave to him. Jesus' work is complete, but the mission of God must continue through his disciples in his physical absence. As such, Jesus offers several petitions concerning the well-being of his disciples (and all who believe).

> "Holy Father, keep them in your name, which you have given me, that they may be one, even as we are one." (v. 11)

> "Keep them from the evil one." (v. 15)

> "Sanctify them in the truth." (v. 17)

> "I do not ask for these only, but also for those who will believe in me through their word, that they may all be one, just as you, Father, are in me, and I in you, that they also may be in us, so that the world may believe that you have sent me." (vv. 20–21)

The nature of these requests become especially relevant in light of the world's inhospitality toward Jesus and his disciples (John 15:18–21; 16:1–4, 32–33). Jesus' concern for the disciples' spiritual well-being is elucidated in his petitions on their behalf. Specifically, Jesus prays that the Father will "keep them" in the Father's "name" for the purpose of oneness (17:11). God's name is often synonymous with his power (e.g., Ps 54:1), but it also involves the revelation of God's being mediated through the Son. Accordingly, Jesus does not pray that his disciples will be taken out of the world, but that they will be "kept" from the "evil one," which most likely refers to the devil (John 17:15).⁴¹ He also prays that the disciples will be sanctified in truth (v. 17), and that all who will believe (v. 20) will be one as he and the Father are one (vv. 20–23). These petitions center on faithfulness to and being set apart by the truth revealed through the Son. The revelation of God mediated to them would serve to unite and consecrate them for service to God (which have ecclesiastical and missional implications).⁴² In summary, Jesus' petitions center on the Father's protection and preservation of the disciples who are left in his absence. As the believers are preserved, the mission of God will be preserved. As they prosper, the mission of God will prosper in the world.

As one turns to 3 John, it is plausible to suggest that the Elder's prayer-wish for Gaius is less explicit and thorough than, but conceptually congruent with Jesus' petition for the well-being of his disciples and their participation in the mission of God. First, in John 17:11 Jesus asks the Father to "keep" his disciples in the Father's "name." This petition involves the preservation of the disciples and their unity with one another. In 3 John 7 Gaius provided hospitality to the emissaries who "have gone out for the sake of the name" (i.e., Jesus'), and by doing so contributed to the unity of the brotherhood and sisterhood of the believing community. Second, Jesus prays in John 17:17 that the Father will "sanctify" the disciples "in the truth." While the Elder does not elaborate on the nature of his prayer for Gaius, he does commend Gaius for "walking in the truth" (vv. 3–4), which involves orthodoxy and orthopraxy, that is, true beliefs and behavior that accords with his beliefs (1 John 1:8; 2:24). The truth that characterized Gaius's life is the practical application of his religious beliefs in showing hospitality to the emissaries. The visible display of truth in Gaius's life justifies the assertion that he is doing well in his soul (3 John 2). As he walks in truth, the mission of God continues. As Gaius prospers

---

41. See references to "the rule of this world" in John 14:30 and 16:11. See also, Matt 6:13; 1 John 2:13–14; 3:12; 5:18–19.

42. Stevick says, "Some of those who had formed the early core of the Johannine church were still present, but a later group had grown up beside them. Evidently in the late first century some tension had developed between two generations in the faith." Stevick, *Jesus and His Own*, 319.

in all things, the emissaries are equipped to prosper in their mission. Third, in John 17:20–23 Jesus prays for the unity of believers, which is especially relevant in light of the divisive situation in 3 John. In addition to using bad language and bringing baseless charges against the Elder, Diotrephes also refused to show hospitality, misused his position, and tried to expel believers from the community.[43] Therefore, it is not difficult to see how Diotrephes's actions, in part, justify the Elder's prayer-wish for Gaius's spiritual and physical well-being (3 John 2) as he contributes to the health, unity, and mission of God in the Johannine community.

Conclusion

Many scholars are convinced that *euchomai* is best understood in 3 John 2 as a standard, ancient health wish. Although possible, this reading is less tenable in light of the overall context of 3 John. It seems more likely that the Elder's introductory remark involves his desire for Gaius's overall well-being *and* his prayer for this desire to come to pass. The Elder not only wished for Gaius's prosperity, but he prayed for it to come to pass for the sake of "the name" and the mission of God. This less conventional but contextual reading accords with the FD, where prayer is prescribed for the fruitfulness of the believing community. In the FD disciples who pray in Jesus' name and on the basis of his indwelling words will perform "greater works" and bear "much fruit." In John 17 Jesus prays for the preservation of his disciples and for the unity of all believers. Perhaps the Elder's prayer-wish and Gaius's prosperity are but a few examples of how God chose to preserve the Johannine emissaries as they carried forth the mission of God in an inhospitable world.

---

43. See Schnackenburg, *The Johannine Epistles*, 297–98.

Chapter 5

Eschatological Prayer in Revelation

THUS FAR, I HAVE examined prayer in the FD, 1 John, and 3 John. In this chapter I will examine petitionary prayer in Revelation 5:8; 6:10; 8:3–4; and 22:20. In particular, this chapter seeks to determine the eschatological function of prayer by examining "the prayers of the saints," the setting in which they are offered, and God's response(s) to them. The analysis that follows will show that, while prayer in the FD is prescribed from an earthly perspective for the continuation of God's mission in Jesus' absence, prayer in Revelation is described from a heavenly perspective[1] and is offered for the completion of God's mission as the martyrs are vindicated, the wicked are judged, and Jesus returns.

Overview of Revelation

The book of Revelation is situated at the end of the New Testament canon as a literary work that is at the same time prophetic and apocalyptic (1:1, 3; 22:6). Written as an instructive epistle to seven churches in Asia Minor, this book is prophetic in the sense that it involves "forth-telling exhortations for the present and foretelling of the future."[2] It is apocalyptic in the sense that it unveils Jesus Christ and reveals that which must soon take place. Comparable

---

1. With the exception of Rev 22:20.
2. See Beale and Campbell, *Revelation*, 6.

to the book of Daniel and other Jewish literature, Revelation is replete with symbolism, visionary experiences, and apocalyptic motifs. Finally, it is eschatological in the sense that it looks forward to God breaking into the systems of this world for a final reckoning.[3] However, it must be noted that Revelation does not merely (or primarily) relate to the distant future; it also draws from the past and addresses John's present and near-future situations. In this document, John the seer provides an account of his visionary experience in the language of his immediate milieu, which anticipates varying degrees of worldly hostility.[4] As such, Revelation provides a dismal portrayal of a fallen world characterized by worldly temptations, Satanic opposition, totalitarian threats, and gross injustices. It is within this historical and literary framework that the topic of prayer will be explored.

The Function of Petitionary Prayer in Revelation

If one defines prayer as direct speech to God, then it may be argued that prayer appears in several forms throughout Revelation including: doxology (1:5b–6; 4:8–9; 5:13; 7:10, 12; 19:1), acclamation (4:11; 5:9, 12), attribution (4:8; 15:3–4; 16:5–7), thanksgiving

---

3. Mounce, *The Book of Revelation*, 3.

4. It is difficult to know for certain the extent to which persecution occurred in John's day. Accepting the viewpoint that persecution was not statewide, but rather localized and sporadic in John's time, Paul Middleton argues that localized persecution could have nonetheless been interpreted as a major experience of persecution. Middleton, *The Violence of the Lamb*, 16–64. Beale suggests that John may view persecution as intensifying in the present as well as in the future. Moreover, several suggestions have been offered concerning the hymnic content of Revelation 4–5. Some assert that the content is patterned after aspects of Second Temple Jewish or early Christian liturgy. Beale and Campbell, *The Book of Revelation*, 28–33. However, Jean-Pierre Ruiz is right in saying that "they are *ad hoc* compositions of the author, who drew upon biblical images in shaping visionary narratives" for the purpose of being read during worship in the seven churches of Asia Minor. He says further, "To deal with the irreconcilably conflicting claims between Christ and the emperor, John's Apocalypse draws from sources that included biblical language and imagery, and from practices of imperial court ceremonial, to equip Christians with resources to resist assimilation." Ruiz, "Revelation," 244.

(11:17–18; 19:7–8), and hallelujahs (19:1, 3, 4, 6).[5] However, this chapter will focus on prayers within the main body of Revelation that are (implicitly or explicitly) petitionary in nature, namely: "the prayers of the saints" (5:8; 8:3–4) and the martyrs' cry for vindication (6:10). I will conclude with an analysis of John's singular petition in the epilogue (22:20). While these prayers are uniquely located within an apocalyptic setting, the analysis below will reveal how they compare with petitionary prayer passages within the FD.

The Prayers of the Saints in Heavenly Perspective: Revelation 5:8

In 5:8 the prayers of the saints are offered subsequent to the Lamb taking the scroll from the right hand of God. As this exchange occurs, the living creatures and the twenty-four elders fall down in worship before him. Stephen Smalley correctly notes that the twenty-four elders rather than the living creatures are those who hold the "harps" and "bowls" (*kitharan kai phialas chrysas*).[6] G. K. Beale says that the elders' role is "modeled after the twenty-four orders of Levites commissioned to give thanks and praise to the Lord in 1 Chron. 25:6–31."[7] In 25:6 music in the house of the LORD was produced with "cymbals, harps, and lyres." These and other instruments are also mentioned in the context of worship in Psalms 33:2; 98:5–6; and 147:7. In Revelation 14:2–3, the voice John heard was like the sound of harpists playing their harps as they sang a "new song" before the living creatures and the throne. In 15:2–3, those who conquered held harps in their hands and sang "the song of Moses" and "the song of the Lamb."

In addition to harps, the twenty-four elders held "golden bowls full of incense"[8] (*phialas chrysas gemousas thymiamatōn*)

---

5. As noted by Ng, "Prayer in Revelation," 120–21; Karris, *Prayer and the New Testament*, 139–55.

6. See Smalley, *The Revelation to John*, 134.

7. Beale and Campbell, *Revelation*, 116. See also 1 Chr 15:16; 16:5; 2 Chr 9:11; Pss 43:4; 81:2; 98:5.

8. Richard Bauckham remarks, "In the earthly sanctuary incense was kept

that symbolize "the prayers of the saints" (*hai proseuchai tōn hagiōn*; Rev 5:8). Here the seer draws the heavenly and earthly temples together in liturgical language. The former is described in Revelation 4–5, whereas the latter seems to relate to the people of God in 11:1. Further, in the Old Testament, incense was often utilized in Israel's worship, particularly within a sacrificial context: it was offered on the altar (Exod 30:1, 6), in the morning and evening (30:7–8), and was accompanied by burnt offerings (Deut 33:10). Jeremy Penner says, "We see that when incense is present, the offering has an anamnestic quality that garnered divine attention" (cf. Lev 2:2, 9, 16; 24:7).[9] Like sacrifice, the offering of incense symbolized the prayers of God's people rising before him as a sweet-smelling aroma.[10] Thus, prayer, incense, and sacrifice are presented together in Psalm 141:2, which states, "Let my prayer be counted as incense before you, and the lifting up of my hands as an evening sacrifice." Accordingly, in the heavenly throne room scene of Revelation 5, "the prayers of the saints" (symbolized by incense) would naturally be viewed as a sweet-smelling aroma when offered to the Lamb/God.[11] For the meantime, it is plausible to suggest that these prayers are being "held in readiness for the time when they will be offered to God in 8:3–4."[12] Notwithstanding, the content of these prayers likely involves petitions for the success of God's mission and the vindication of God's people who have been slaughtered for their Christian witness.[13] As the Lamb

---

in the golden bowls on 'the bread of the Presence' (cf. Exod. 25.29; Lev. 24:7)." Bauckham, "Prayer in the Book of Revelation," 254.

9. Penner, *Patterns of Daily Prayer*, 42. He says further that the potency of the sacrifice was thought to provide "added weight to the performance of prayer."

10. Aune, "Magic in Early Christianity," 358.

11. Bauckham does not view the prayers of the saints as being offered to God in Revelation 5:8. He notes instead, "To be offered, the incense had to be burned on the golden altar. At this point in chapter 5, however, the prayers of the saints are simply being held in readiness for the time when they will be offered to God in 8:3–4." Bauckham, "Prayer in the Book of Revelation," 254.

12. See Bauckham, "Prayer in the Book of Revelation," 254.

13. Blount, *Revelation*, 113.

laid down his life for the saints,[14] so the saints were willing to lay down their lives for the cause of the Lamb and the mission of God. The liturgical actions of the elders on behalf of the saints anticipate a divine response that will be examined below.[15]

As one turns to the Old Testament background, incense was not only offered at specific times, it also consisted of a specific composition that was considered holy to the LORD (Exod 30:34–35, 37). As such, "unauthorized incense" was strictly prohibited (Exod 30:9). Therefore, it follows that "the prayers of the saints" in Revelation 5:8 (and in 8:3–4) would naturally be compatible with those prescribed by the Lamb. The FD authorizes prayer to God in

---

14. In Rev 5:9 Jesus is considered worthy to take the scroll and break its seals because he was slain and ransomed people for God with his own blood. It is helpful to read verses 9 and 12 against the background of the Day of Atonement and the Passover, both of which serve as reminders of salvation and judgment. Paige Patterson says, "In the Day of Atonement prescription, the blood of sacrificial goats is carried into the holy of holies and sprinkled on the mercy seat. Interposed between the just demands of the law of God and the sinful high priest (Lev 16:15–17). The Passover takes the blood of the lamb slain by each family and sprinkles it on the door facing so that the death angel passes over (Exod 12:1–13)." Patterson, *Revelation*, 168–69. Smalley points to Isaiah 53:7 (LXX), which describes the Servant of God "as being led to the slaughter 'like a lamb' (ὡς πρόβατον ἐπὶ σφαγὴν ἤχθη . . .)." Smalley, *The Revelation to John*, 136. The effect of the Lamb's death is emancipation from sin for the peoples of the world and heaven and earth respond in worshipful prostration and adoration (Rev 5:9–11). Like the people of Israel (Exod 19:6), the redeemed of Rev 5:9–10 shall be "a kingdom and priests" to God. Keener, *Revelation*, 189. Beasley-Murray notes, "As the passover lambs were slain for Israel's release from sin, and thereby made possible the nation's emancipation from the Egyptian slavery to become the covenant people of God in the promised land, so the death of the Lamb of God, coupled with his resurrection, brought to men emancipation from sin's slavery, that they might become members in the race drawn from all nations, a company of kings and priests to God in the new age." Beasley-Murray, *The Book of Revelation*, 127. As seen in Revelation, Jesus, the slain Lamb, initiates a final exodus from sin and the systems of the world. In doing so the righteous are saved and the wicked are judged.

15. Gordon Fee views these prayers as reminders for John's audience that in the midst of suffering, their prayers are being heard in heaven. Fee, *Revelation*, 84. Leon Morris notes, "On earth the saints are despised and accounted as of no importance. In heaven their prayers are precious, being brought into the very presence of God himself, while the bowls in which they are offered are golden." Morris, *Revelation*, 99.

Jesus' name with the assurance that Jesus himself will do whatever one asks for (John 14:13-14). As I have noted in a previous work, "The name of Jesus encapsulates his nature and earthly mission, which involved performing the works of the Father, offering salvation to all who believe, and bringing glory to the Father."[16] Thus, the content of prayer is shaped by one's belief in Jesus and fidelity to his saving cause in the earth. Accordingly, Jesus says in John 15:7 that if his words abide in the believer, then one may ask for whatever he or she wishes and it will be done for them. In the case of 14:12-14, the believer will perform "greater works." In the context of the 15:5 and v. 8, the believer will bear "much fruit." In short, answered prayer contributes to the Johannine community's spiritual health and numerical growth as they carry forth the mission of God in Jesus' physical absence.

Moreover, while prayer in John 14:13-14 and 15:7 is offered for the *continuation* of God's mission, "the prayers of the saints" in Revelation 5:8 are held in anticipation of the *completion* of God's mission. Concerning the latter, the sweet-smelling, persuasive force of "the prayers of the saints" is due to the nature of their content, which most plausibly consists of their concern for the mission of God and those who have given their lives for it (thus anticipating Rev 6:9-10).[17] Yet the nature of "the prayers of the saints" and the heavenly setting in which they are offered serve to persuade the saints on earth that their prayers will be attended to. In 5:8 John hoists his audience from their historical situation into the throne room of heaven in order to symbolically elucidate the height to which their prayers had risen. Even though the saints in John's day were decades removed from the historical Jesus, their prayers ascend into heaven like sweet-smelling incense. The same Jesus who bids farewell to his disciples in the FD remains

---

16. Adams, *Prayer in John's Farewell Discourse*, 88-89.

17. Grant Osborne says, "There is probably a connection between these prayers [5:8] and the prayers of 6:9-11 and 8:3-4. . . .The outpouring of the trumpet judgments (chaps. 8-9) is God's response to these prayers (8:3-5). This is startling: the judgments of the seals, trumpets, and bowls are in part God's answer to the prayers of the saints." Osborne, *Revelation*, 259.

functionally accessible to the saints who carry forth his mission in the world.

Prayer as the Martyrs' Cry for Vindication: Revelation 6:9–11

In Revelation 6:9 the fifth seal is opened, and in contradistinction to seals 1–4 (Rev 6:1–8), no apocalyptic woe is announced and no summons is offered (*erchou*). Instead, emphasis is placed on the cries (*ekraxan*) of the souls who had been slain for the word of God and for their Christian witness. With the background of the FD in mind, "greater works" provoked great opposition. "Much fruit" eventuated much worldly hatred (John 15:18–25; 16:1–4). This was the case for some believers before John's day and beyond his day. In Revelation 6:9, he saw "under the altar the souls of those who had been slain for the word of God." The term *altar* (*thysiastērion*) appears throughout Revelation (6:9; 8:3; 8:5; 9:13; 11:1; 14:18; 16:7). Elsewhere in the New Testament this term is used mainly in reference to the altar of burnt offering at the Jerusalem temple (e.g., Matt 23:18–20; Luke 11:51; 1 Cor 10:18; Heb 7:13). In the context of Revelation 6:9, some see the term as referring to the heavenly altar of burnt offering. However, it is possible that this heavenly altar blends the altar of burnt offering and the altar of incense together. There is no reason why in John's vision the two should not blend together into one.[18] Notwithstanding, Smalley remarks,

> In the Levitical cult some of the blood of the victim, which in Judaic thought contained its 'life' . . . , was poured out at the *foot* of the altar (Lev 4.7). In the same way it may be understood at this point that the life ("soul") of the Christian martyrs, whose blood was poured out as a libation to God (Phil. 2.17; 2 Tim. 4.6), has been laid for safe-keeping at the base of the altar of burnt offering in heaven (cf. 4 Macc. 6.29).[19]

---

18. See Mounce, *The Book of Revelation*, 146; Tabb, *All Things New*, 141.
19. Smalley, *The Revelation to John*, 158.

Although some scholars do not view the martyrs as real people, Beale is correct in saying, "The petitioning saints are those who have been exalted to a heavenly state, now separated from the sinful influences of the world."[20] As such, their literal[21] cry of the slain for vindication is reminiscent of the figurative cry of Abel's blood from the ground. In 1 John 3:12 the author reinforces the intention behind Cain's murder of Abel. Cain was of the "evil one" and murdered his brother because Abel's deeds were "righteous." In verse 13 the author views Cain's sinful actions as paradigmatic of the world's hatred of the believing community. With this example in mind, it is not hard to see how the righteous and faithful witness of the martyrs (in Revelation 6:9) would have incited bloodshed from the world. Their commitment to the word of God and faithfulness to Jesus would naturally draw hostility from those who stood against the message they proclaimed and the righteous lives they lived. After all, the church in Revelation is presented as a "witnessing church."[22] As noted above, the theme of bloodshed is seen in Revelation 5:9–10 where John sees the slain Lamb who ransomed people for God from every tribe and language and people and nation.

The extensive scope of Jesus' cross-death is also highlighted in John 3:16 and 1 John 2:2. Yet the fundamental basis for Jesus' death is love for the world in general and for his disciples in particular. Jesus says in John 15:13, "Greater love has no one than this, that someone lay down his life for his friends." In turn, believers are required to imitate Jesus in sacrificial acts of love toward one another in the community (John 13:34–35; 1 John 3:16). As indicated in 1 John 3:21, those who lay down their lives for their brothers and sisters can have confidence before God in prayer (*parrēsian echomen pros ton theon*). Such loving, ethical behavior is not the forensic basis of their right-standing before God, but is the corollary of believing in his name and abiding in his love. But those

---

20. Beale and Campbell, *The Book of Revelation*, 392.

21. Contra Bauckham ("Prayer in the Book of Revelation," 261), who does not see their prayers as a literal description.

22. See Osborne, *Revelation*, 285.

who lay down their lives for their brothers and sisters must also be willing to give up their lives for Jesus and his mission in the earth. In turn, prayers that arise from the altar of sacrificial obedience to God are a sweet-smelling aroma to his nostrils.

Furthermore, in Revelation 6:10 the martyrs offer the loud prayer-cry, "O Sovereign Lord, holy and true, how long before you will judge and avenge our blood on those who dwell on the earth?" Here the martyrs' cry elucidates their desire for justice and a timely response. However, it must be noted that their cry does not arise from personal agitation,[23] but from the missional opposition they faced.[24] They stood fast in the face of worldly hostility and paid the ultimate price. Accordingly, Beale says that the saints' cry for vindication is "a desire that God demonstrate before the whole world that they were right and their persecutors in the wrong. This is to be done by God justifying them in the heavenly court by overturning the wrong verdict on them rendered by the earthly courts (cf. Luke 18:1–8)."[25] In response to their petitions, the saints "were each given" (divine passive) a white robe[26] and told to rest "a little longer" (*chronon mikron*) until the number of deaths of their fellow servants and their brothers should be complete (Rev 6:11). In short, they are told to wait "a little longer" because more faithful saints must die before justice will be served.[27]

---

23. Osborne sees their cry as "an imprecatory prayer for vengeance" (cf. Pss 6:3; 74:10; 79:5; 80:4). He says, "The connection between martyrdom and judgment is appropriate, for one of the primary emphases in the book is *lex talionis* (the law of retribution), defending why God has to judge evil humanity." Osborne, *Revelation*, 284.

24. Beale views the ones who had been "slain" as "all saints who suffer for the sake of their faith." Beale and Campbell, *Revelation*, 133.

25. Beale and Campbell, *The Book of Revelation*, 393.

26. Mounce says that white robes are "symbols of blessedness and purity." Mounce, *The Book of Revelation*, 149. Beale notes, "The metaphor of white robes connotes the idea of a purity which has resulted from persevering faith tested by the refining fire of tribulation (see on 3:4–5). Robes are given not only as a reward for purity of faith but as a heavenly declaration of the saints' purity or righteousness and an annulling of the guilty verdict rendered on them by the world." Beale and Campbell, *Revelation*, 135.

27. For examples of divine vengeance in the OT, see 2 Sam 3:28–29; 2 Chr

Eschatological Prayer in Revelation

The Old Testament is replete with examples of waiting for God to act in salvation and judgment. For example, Habakkuk 1:2 states, "O Lord, how long shall I cry for help, and you will not hear?" In this instance, the petitioner suffers anguish as he questions why God has not responded to his cries for help. As indicated in Habakkuk 2:3, one must wait patiently for God to act in his timing. Consider also the following examples from the Psalms:

> Wait for the Lord; be strong, and let your heart take courage; wait for the Lord! (27:14)

> I wait for the Lord, my soul waits, and in his word I hope; my soul waits for the Lord more than watchmen for the morning, more than watchmen for the morning. (130:5–6)

Finally, the psalmist cries out concerning the anger of the Lord:

> "How long, O Lord? Will you be angry forever? Will your jealousy burn like fire? Pour out your anger on the nations that do not know you, and on the kingdoms that do not call upon your name!" (79:5–6)

The theme of waiting on God/Jesus also appears in the FG.[28] Upon hearing that Lazarus was ill (John 11:3), Jesus stayed where he was two more days (11:6) before approaching the tomb and vocalizing his prayer for Lazarus's resurrection (11:41–42). The negative emotional effect of Jesus' delay is seen in Mary's statement, "Lord, if you had been here, my brother would not have died" (11:32). In the FD the theme of waiting is elucidated in the context of Jesus' disappearance and reappearance.[29]

24:22; Pss 7:6–9; 58:3–11; 79:5–7; 109:7–20; 112:8; 119:154–58; Jer 15:15; Amos 7:16–17 (Smalley, *The Revelation to John*, 161). Further, John Christopher Thomas and Frank Macchia note, "Thus, as these souls wait, their earlier cry would be understood to expand to include the prayer for justice and vindication both for them and for those who will complete them. And John and his hearers wait as well." Thomas and Macchia, *Revelation*, 162.

28. See elsewhere in the NT, 1 Thess 1:10; Jas 5:7–11; 2 Pet 3:12; Jude 21.

29. The following two paragraphs are a paraphrased summary of a section from my work. See Adams, *Prayer in John's Farewell Discourse*, 150–54. This paragraph also includes several quotations from other scholars that I cited in this work.

> A little while, and you will see me no longer; and again a little while, and you will see me. (John 16:16)

Carson rightly views the "little while" when the disciples will not see him as referring to his death and the second "little while" statement as referring to his return in resurrection.[30] In 16:20 Jesus offers forthright assurance that, while the world rejoices (*kosmos charēsetai*), the disciples will experience sorrow. They will indeed weep and lament. The term *thrēnēsete* ("to lament") appears only here (v. 20), while the verb *klausete* ("to weep") appears in John 11:33; 20:11, 13, and 15 as a deep emotional expression by Mary in the context of death. In 16:21 the Evangelist presents an image that illustrates the nature of the situation they are facing:

> When a woman is giving birth, she has sorrow because her hour has come, but when she has delivered the baby, she no longer remembers the anguish, for joy that a human being has been born into the world.

This analogy concerning the emotional state of the mother would prove relevant for the disciples as they experienced sorrow over not seeing Jesus. However, like a woman giving birth, the disciples' sorrow would eventually turn to joy as they anticipate seeing Jesus again. In that day, they will approach the Father via Jesus' name and obtain whatever they request. As a result of their asking and receiving, they will experience the fullness of joy (16:23–24).

Furthermore, in Matthew 24:6–8, Jesus relates various eschatological woes to the beginning of the "birth pains" of a woman in labor (also Mark 13:8). As time passes, the pains will increase in frequency and duration. Certainly, being delivered up for tribulation, being put to death, and being hated by all nations for Jesus'

---

30. Carson, *The Gospel according to John*, 543. John Ashton notes further that the repeated phrase "in a little while" (16:16–19) conveys a second or spiritual level of meaning. He says that it is on this level of understanding that we "must adopt the perspective of John's hearers or the reader of his Gospel, who know the resurrection has already happened. Heirs to the promise, enjoying as they read or listen to the life that Jesus came to bring, they have nevertheless retained . . . some belief in his eventual return." Ashton, *Understanding the Fourth Gospel*, 464–65.

name's sake (Matt 24:9; see also Mark 13:12–13; Luke 21:16) is congruent with the expectation for death via persecution in Revelation 6:11. In the process of bearing witness about Jesus to the nations, the saints will be put to death by the nations.[31] This is a painful, sorrowful process that must take place before the faithful receive their full reward. As such, eschatological joy is delayed until the full number of deaths has been completed. Prayer is offered, but the fulfilment of the martyrs' cry is postponed. From an earthly viewpoint, this grim reality might naturally provoke temporary sorrow among the faithful. But from the victorious outlook of Revelation, joy is sure to come as the martyrs' prayers are answered, justice is carried out, the dead are resurrected, and the mission of God is completed.[32] Death via martyrdom will occur for many, but sacrificial acts of obedience for the cause of Christ will be rewarded and vindicated.

In Revelation 6:9–11 the rhetorical force of prayer comes into sharper focus. The prayer-cry of the martyrs elucidates their desire for divine justice to be executed against their overpowering oppressors. As in Jewish and early Christian literature, prayer in 6:10 functions as the means by which the oppressed resist their oppressor through superior, divine aid.[33] Accordingly, their cry functions as a sort of eschatological resistance against those who oppose the mission of God (whether Roman or any totalitarian threat). The martyrs did not raise worldly weapons against their oppressors. Instead, after being put to death for their verbal witness for Jesus, they raised their cry to the "Sovereign Lord, holy and true" (6:10) who, in turn, guarantees vindication before the world. The martyrs' cry and God's response to them would naturally provide encouragement for the saints in John's day and for believers throughout history who are facing eschatological labor

31. See Fee, *Revelation*, 97.

32. Beale remarks accordingly, "The assurance that God will unquestionably punish the evil world becomes a motivation for Christians to persevere in their witness through suffering on earth, knowing that they are key players in helping establish the kingdom in the same ironic fashion as their Lord (e.g., see on 1:6, 9; 5:5–10)." Beale and Campbell, *Revelation*, 136.

33. DeSilva, *Seeing Things John's Way*, 290.

pains. The answer to their prayer-cries may be delayed, but their requests will not be denied.

Prayer and Eschatological Judgment: Revelation 8:3–4

In 8:1 the seventh seal is opened, which gives way to silence in heaven for about half an hour. This silence is reminiscent of Habakkuk 2:20, Zephaniah 1:7, and Zechariah 2:13. But what is the meaning of silence in the present context? It is possible that this short period is in reference to the time required for incense to be offered in the temple.[34] In Luke 1:9–10 the offering of incense and prayer are linked, which may suggest silence in heaven as God listens to the prayers of his people.[35] More likely, it is the position advanced by Mounce who remarks, "It is a dramatic pause that makes even more impressive the judgments about to fall upon the earth."[36] During this time of silence "the seven angels" were given seven trumpets[37] (Rev 8:2), which anticipates the events that follow in 8:6–9:21 and 11:15–19. In 8:3 "another angel" came and stood at the altar with a golden censer.[38] He "was given" (divine passive) much incense to offer "with the prayers of all the saints." Here the angel carries out priestly duties in the heavenly temple as he offers the prayers on the golden altar before the throne of God. However, while the angel offers the prayers of all the saints to God in heaven, the saints who form the communal temple on

---

34. See Bauckham, "Prayer in the Book of Revelation," 256; Koester, *Revelation*, 434.

35. Witherington, *Revelation*, 139.

36. Mounce, *The Book of Revelation*, 170.

37. Mounce calls these "eschatological trumpets" that "herald the day of God's wrath." Mounce, *The Book of Revelation*, 173. See also Exod 19:16; Isa 27:13; Joel 2:1; Zeph 1:16; Zech 9:14.

38. Margaret Barker contends, "The angel with the incense is not 'another' angel but the Lamb himself, the Mighty Angel, who has been enthroned as the LORD and now prepares to emerge from heaven." Barker, *Revelation of Jesus Christ*, 170.

Eschatological Prayer in Revelation

earth (Rev 3:12; 11:1-2) have direct priestly access to God through the mediation of the Lamb.[39]

Whereas in 5:8 the seer speaks of "the prayers of the saints," in 8:3 the scope of prayer is widened to include "the prayers of all the saints." John Christopher Thomas and Frank Macchia note, "In 6:10 it is the cries of those who had been slaughtered that are heard; here it is the prayers of all the saints. The broadening of the scope of the prayers offered has increased to include not only those who have been martyred but also those who are alive."[40] In this reading the saints on earth share the same concern to see the justice of God and the vindication of the martyrs carried out. Smalley does not limit the prayers to the specific concerns of the martyrs in 6:9. In his view, they may refer to "petitions for judgment on sin and injustice in general."[41] It is also possible that "the prayers of all the saints" include those unrelated to God's judgment but nonetheless related to the advancement of his mission of God and the salvation of the world (John 14:13-14; 15:7, 16). Notwithstanding, it is difficult to escape the conclusion that "the prayers of all the saints" relate in some fashion to the vindication of the martyrs as God responds in acts of severe judgment (see also "The Song of Moses," Deut 32:1-43).

There are two possible options with respect to the statement, "and he was given much incense to offer with the prayers of all the saints" (Rev 8:3; see also verse 4). The first option says that the incense is offered *with* the prayers of the saints. The second option says that the incense *is* the prayers of the saints.[42] The first reading conveys the idea that incense ascended alongside their prayers to God, thereby implying some sort of divine assistance. Osborne posits the idea that incense "bore the prayers of the saints up to God."[43] Esther Yue L. Ng's suggestion that incense may func-

---

39. Koester, "Rethinking the Ethics of John," 390.

40. Thomas and Macchia, *Revelation*, 177.

41. Smalley, *The Revelation to John*, 215.

42. See Beasley-Murray, *The Book of Revelation*, 150-51; Mounce, *The Book of Revelation*, 174; Osborne, *Revelation*, 344-45.

43. Osborne, *Revelation*, 345.

tion as divine assistance by the Holy Spirit on the saints' behalf is not convincing.[44] The second reading is congruent with Revelation 5:8 where the incense is identified as the prayers of the saints. Similarly, it may be that the prayers of 8:3–4 are acceptable to God because they are offered in accordance with his will. However, with 6:9–10 in mind, it is also plausible to suggest that the prayers in 8:3 are acceptable because they rise from sacrificial obedience to Jesus' commandments and his mission.[45]

In Revelation 12:17 the beast makes war against "those who keep the commandments of God and hold to the testimony of Jesus." In 14:12 the saints are identified as "those who keep the commandments of God and their faith in Jesus." In short, the saints lost their lives because of their faith in Jesus, obedience to his words, and loyalty to his mission. They sacrificed their lives for the one who offered the ultimate sacrifice for them and their prayers rose before God as a sweet-smelling aroma. In these examples we hear echoes from Jesus' prayer in John 17. For example, the martyred saints,

- knew God, the only true God, and Jesus Christ whom God sent (v. 3);
- glorified God on earth, having accomplished the work that he gave them to do (v. 4);
- manifested his name (v. 6);
- received the words that Jesus gave them (vv. 8, 14);
- were hated by the world and were sent into the world (vv. 14, 18);
- were protected (spiritually) from the evil one (vv. 12, 15);
- were unified in their word and witness (vv. 21–23).

In Revelation 8:3, the "prayers of all the saints" are explicitly linked to the completion of God's mission through acts of judgment upon the wicked. Their prayers are presented "on the golden altar before

---

44. See Ng, "Prayer in Revelation," 133.
45. See Beale and Campbell, *Revelation*, 168.

the throne" (*epi to thysiastērion to chrysoun to enōpion tou thronou*). As this occurred, the smoke of the incense and their prayers rose to God from the hand of the angel (v. 4). Presumably this is the same altar noted in Revelation 6:9, which likely recalls the cry of the martyrs for divine justice (hence, a blending of the altar of incense and the altar of burnt offering). The prayers of the saints have ascended before God with incense, and now the answer to their prayers will descend in judgment. In a scene reminiscent of Sinai (Exod 19:16-19), the angel took the censer, filled it with fire from the altar, and threw it on the earth, which resulted in "peals of thunder, rumblings, flashes of lightning, and an earthquake" (Rev 8:5; see also 4:5). Taken together, fire from the altar being thrown to the earth and these cataclysmic events signal the judgement of God in the earth. Smalley points out, "Fire falling from heaven is a regular symbol of divine judgment in biblical literature (cf. Gen. 19.24; Exod. 19.18; 2 Kings 1.10, 12, 14; Job 1.16; Ps. 11.6; 18.8; Luke 9.54. Heb. 12.29; according to Rev. 1.14; 2.18 the eyes of the exalted Son of man 'flame like fire')."[46] Francis Moloney does not view "fire" strictly in terms of judgment that befalls the wicked in the last days. Rather, he points out that episodes in the Synoptic Gospels "accompany the death and resurrection of Jesus with the same effects that the casting down of the censer full of fire generates (Matt. 27:45-54; 28:1-4; Mark 15:33-39; Luke 23:44-45)." He concludes, "The death and resurrection of Jesus will bring a fire that judges; some will be condemned and others will be saved. This is the 'fire from the altar,' thrown down upon the earth."[47] Notwithstanding, each of the three series of judgements move history toward the same goal: the completion of God's mission in the earth.

Bauckham sees a causal relationship between the prayers of the saints and the judgements that ensue from "the golden altar" (*to thysiastērion to chrysoun*). In particular, he traces a link from the altar of Revelation 8:3 to the altar associated with the sixth trumpet blast in 9:13.[48] As judgement follows the opening of the

46. Smalley, *The Revelation to John*, 216.
47. Moloney, *The Apocalypse of John*, 132-34.
48. Bauckham, "Prayer in the Book of Revelation," 258.

seventh seal (leading to the seven trumpets), so judgement also occurs at the sounding of the sixth trumpet via the four angels (9:14-15). Accordingly, in 14:14-16 the grain harvest occurs wherein souls are harvested from the world into the kingdom of God. By contrast, in 14:17-21 the grape harvest occurs when the angel in charge of the fire commands another angel to put his sickle to the grape harvest. It is possible that the angel in charge of the fire in 14:18 is the same one in 8:3-4 who, after offering the prayers of all the saints, cast fire from the altar to the earth (v. 5). Bauckham says concerning these events,

> It is striking and important to note that, of the two images of eschatological grain harvest and the eschatological grape harvest, only the second is connected with the prayers of the saints by the reference to the altar of incense. And if we further observe that the unfinished image of the vintage is completed in 19:15, where the identity of the one who will tread the wine press is revealed (cf. 19:11-16), then we can conclude that the prayers of the saints are for the coming of the Lord Jesus to judge his enemies and to deliver his people.[49]

In 5:8 the elders hold "golden bowls full of incense," which are "the prayers of the saints." In 15:7 the four living creatures give the seven angels "seven golden bowls." In this instance instead of being full of "the prayers of the saints," the golden bowls are "full of the wrath of God." What follows are the seven final bowl judgments poured out upon the earth. The finality of these judgments is reported in 16:17, which states, "The seventh angel poured out his bowl into the air, and a loud voice came out of the temple, from the throne, saying, 'It is done!'" Moreover, in Revelation 18-19:4 the great oracle of judgment against Babylon is explicated in further detail. The city guilty of the shedding of innocent bloodshed falls under the power and wrath of God.[50] At last, the martyr's blood is

---

49. Bauckham, "Prayer in the Book of Revelation," 258.

50. Paul Middleton says, "John has no concern for the welfare of the inhabitants of the earth; his only concern is that his churches note the terrible fate that is in store for the followers of the Beast, and interpret any present or

vindicated and God's judgment is completed.[51] As seen in Revelation 5:8, 6:10, and 8:3-4, John presents prayer as the means by which the saints participate in this eschatological endeavor.

Prayer and the Coming of Jesus: Revelation 22:20

The final prayer of Revelation is located in 22:20 and serves as a fitting climax. In Revelation 21-22 John describes the creation of the new heaven and new earth, the descent of the New Jerusalem, and the breath-taking river of life that flows from the throne of God. Satan has been cast into the lake of burning sulfur (20:10), the dead have been judged (20:11-15), and the saints are now depicted as dwelling and reigning with God forever (22:3-5). In 22:7 Jesus remarks, "And behold, I am coming soon. Blessed is the one who keeps the words of the prophecy of this book." In verse 12 Jesus expands the reminder of his coming by noting that he will reward individuals on the basis of what they have done. In response to the beatitudes of Jesus and John (vv. 7, 14), "the Spirit and the Bride say, 'Come'" (v. 17). The invitation continues, "And let the one who hears say, 'Come.' And let the one who is thirsty come; let the one who desires take the water of life without price." To whom are these invitations offered? To Christ? To believers? To the world? Robert Mounce is right in saying, "It is possible to take the first two as requests directed to Christ for his return and the second two as invitations to the world to come and take of the water of life. It is more likely that the first half of the verse should be interpreted by the second, and that the entire invitation is addressed to the world."[52]

However, in verse 20 the emphasis shifts to the coming of Jesus. In response to Jesus' promise to come "quickly/soon" in 22:20a, John says "Amen" and then presents the vocative request, "Come,

---

potential difficulty, pressure, or persecution in light of a far worse fate that lies ahead if they do no repent." Middleton, *The Violence of the Lamb*, 176.

51. See the helpful discussion on "The God Whose Patience Has an End" in DeSilva, *Seeing Things John's Way*, 172-73.

52. Mounce, *The Book of Revelation*, 409.

Lord Jesus!" (22:20b). In Revelation 6:1, 3, 5, and 7, the living creatures summon the apocalyptic horses to "Come" (the imperative, *Erchou*). It must be noted that nowhere in the Christian literature is one encouraged to command God. Therefore, when utilized in the context of 22:20b, this term is employed as an entreaty wherein John simply bids Jesus do what he promised.[53] But what does his coming involve? Some have suggested this prayer is set in a eucharistic setting that bids Jesus to come via eucharistic presence. Brian Blount remarks, "One can easily imagine members of John's churches, after just listening to a reading of his work and then hearing this petition, now moving directly into the meal, where the cultic presence of the Lord would encourage participants to trust in the imminent coming of his eschatological presence."[54] Didache 10:6 utilizes this prayer in a eucharistic dialogue that states, "Let grace come, and let this world pass away. Hosanna to the Son of David. If any one is holy let him come (to the Eucharist); if any one is not, let him repent. Maranatha. Amen."[55] Similarly, in 1 Corinthians 16:22 the Aramaic prayer, *Marana tha* ("Our Lord, come!") is preceded by the warning, "If anyone has no love for the Lord, let him be accursed."

Furthermore, John's prayer is preceded by gracious invitations and by dire warnings (Rev 22:17-19). While some scholars are right to view John's prayer in light of the final return of Christ at the end of the age,[56] given the overall context of Revelation, it is best to view this prayer also in terms of Jesus' coming in salvation and judgment in John's day, throughout history, and at the consummation of history through acts of salvation and judgement.[57]

---

53. See Bauckham, "Prayer in the Book of Revelation," 267.

54. Blount, *Revelation*, 416.

55. Gonzalez, *The Didache*.

56. See Ladd, *A Commentary on the Revelation of John*, 296; Giesen, *Die Offenbarung des Johannes*, 80; Mounce, *The Book of Revelation*, 410; Beale and Campbell, *Revelation*, 527.

57. Beale also leaves room for future returns leading up to the final return. He remarks, "That is, Jesus assures the churches about the truth of the complete vision by guaranteeing that His final advent, which He promised at His first coming, will soon occur and thus bring to completion what He has

Smalley says, "In Johannine thought the idea [of the coming of Jesus] relates to the advent of the exalted Christ in the church and to the world at any time, as well as the end-time."[58] In John 14:3, the Evangelist indicates that Jesus will "come again" to take the disciples to himself, that where he is they may be also. This coming occurred via the Paraclete upon his glorification (John 14:18, 23), but will also occur with finality at the *parousia*.[59] As John the Evangelist prescribes prayer in Jesus' name for the *continuation* of God's mission (John 14:13–14; 15:16; 16:23), John the seer summons Jesus to come again in order to *complete* (John 17:4) God's mission in the church and the world. Besides, Jesus' final advent is the climax of prophecy and history.[60]

---

revealed throughout the book. It is conceivable that also in mind are Jesus' future prior comings which culminate in the last coming (see on 1:7; 2:5; 3:3, 11; 22:7, 12)." Beale and Campbell, *Revelation*, 527.

58. Smalley, *The Revelation to John*, 585. David Aune notes, "John has appended the prophecy of Jesus in v 20a to the response of the Christian community represented by the author in v 20b, not specifically as a reinforcement or sanction for the curses in vv 18–19 but more generally as a sanction for the total message of Revelation." Aune, *Revelation 1–5*, 1236.

59. Culpepper sees the promise of Jesus' coming as not referring to the second advent but to the post-Easter experiences. Culpepper, *The Gospel and Letters of John*, 210. Moloney agrees by noting that "too much of Jesus' earlier preaching has insisted on the present gift of life to the believer for the reader to collapse Jesus' promise of 14:3 into a time scheme totally conditioned by an end-time eschatology." Moloney, *Glory Not Dishonor*, 34. Dodd, who views chapter 14 as the Johannine reinterpretation of the church's current belief concerning the departure and return of Christ, interprets Jesus' statement about "coming again" in the sense that: (a) Christ will continue his mighty works in the disciples (14:12); (b) the Paraclete will dwell in them (14:15–17); (c) they will live by virtue of the living Christ (14:19); and (d) they will continue in personal interchange of agape with him (14:21). Dodd, *The Interpretation of the Fourth Gospel*, 395.

60. Thomas and Macchia note, "This emphatic promise clearly picks up on the words of warning by the resurrected Jesus that he will come in judgment to those churches who do not hear (and keep) what the Spirit is saying to them in the seven prophetic messages and the words of the prophecy as a whole. These words also emphasize the way in which the consummation of this promise is the consummation of all the eschatological promises, of all prophetic words— for in a very real way, the return of Jesus is indeed the climax of prophecy, even of history itself!" Thomas and Macchia, *Revelation*, 402.

Conclusion

This chapter examined petitionary prayer in Revelation 5:8; 6:10; 8:3–4; and 22:20 for the purpose of ascertaining its eschatological function. This analysis also placed Revelation in conversation with prayer passages within the FD in order to discern how these documents provide a fuller picture concerning the function of Johannine prayer. While they differ in many respects, both documents, in their own unique ways, link petitionary prayer to the mission of God. In the FD prayer is prescribed from an earthly perspective for the continuation of God's mission. In Revelation prayer is described from a heavenly perspective for its role in the completion of God's mission. John hoists his audience from their worldly situation into the throne room of heaven in order to symbolically elucidate the height to which their prayers had risen. Although many saints will fall by the sword and fall prey to worldly opposition, their prayers will rise from the sacrificial altar of their lives as a sweet-smelling aroma to heaven.

Accordingly, prayer in Revelation stands for the saints' resistance against evil and injustice, their refusal to be silenced, and their holy stubbornness to accept things the way they are. Prayer turns victims into victors and slaughtered sheep into roaring lions. The "prayers of the saints" call for the eschatological inbreaking of divine assistance against the oppressive systems of this world where injustice seems to have the upper hand. Prayer that rises to God ensures that Babylon falls to the ground. As "the prayers of the saints" are spoken, the power of totalitarian governments is sure to be broken. In the final analysis, prayer in Revelation summons Jesus to come again in order to complete his mission in the church and the world.

Chapter 6

Contemporary Implications of Johannine Prayer

THE PREVIOUS CHAPTERS OF this book examined the Johannine literature in order to discern how prayer functions in this ancient tradition. As such, I have focused exclusively on the various Johannine texts without regard to contemporary application. However, as mentioned in the introduction of this book, it is my contention that the Johannine Scriptures are not merely ancient documents to be read and interpreted, they contain timeless truths that are to be applied and obeyed. Therefore, my aim in this final chapter centers on highlighting specific principles from the previous chapters that have direct relevance for our lives as we anticipate Jesus' second advent.

The Purpose of Prayer

While prayer may be defined in a number of ways, it is perhaps most simply understood as communication with God. It is the means by which we draw close to him and make our requests known. Prayer provides a safe place, a place of existential comfort and divine consolation. Through it we offer open and honest communication with the God of all creation. Through it we offer words of concern, complaint, confession, contrition, and other forms of address to the thrice holy God of the Jewish-Christian Scriptures. Accordingly, Petro Bilaniuk defines Christian prayer as,

> a mysterious and loving gift of God the Father through the Son and in the Holy Spirit, which comes to us as a supernatural call in faith, hope, and love, and develops into an intimate and personal polylogue with the Tri-Personal God, which includes His praises, petitions, and thanksgiving, and is the expression of a participation in His inner life, light, and love, and which ascends from us to God the Father, as to the Head of the Divine Family, through the Son and in the Holy Spirit.[1]

Thus, prayer is nothing if it is not relational. But prayer is more than just human communication with the divine. For all intents and purposes, we pray because we assume that there are practical benefits from doing so. Put simply, we pray because we believe that prayer works. As Christians we rightly insist that God hears our prayers and responds in acts of financial provision, physical protection, and a host of other personal benefits. But we must proceed with caution. While it is common for Christians to think of prayer in such terms, we must remember that the purpose of prayer extends well beyond our own immediate needs. The Johannine tradition calls for us to pray for those around us and for those beyond us. It compels us to intercede for the physical and spiritual well-being of our brothers and sisters. It leaves us with no choice but to offer petitions for the good of our communities, the growth of our churches, and the salvation of the world. In this chapter I will explore how Johannine prayer fleshes out in more detail. But first attention will be given to the promises and prerequisites to answered prayer.

The Promises and Prerequisites of Prayer

The Johannine literature is strikingly clear that God answers prayer. Through prayer we have the opportunity to perform

---

1. Bilaniuk, "Some Remarks," 214.

"greater works" and bear "much fruit" for the glory of the Father (John 14:13–14; 15:7–8). However, as stunning as these truths are, they must be contextualized. Jesus is not giving us a blank check to ask for whatever we want without qualification. We must remember that using Jesus' name in prayer does not cast a magic spell on God that persuades him to act in our behalf. To be sure, there are conditions to answered prayer, but these conditions are on Jesus' terms, not on ours. To put it another way, they are according to his sacred will, not according to our carnal desires.

With this in mind, the FD says that prayer is to be offered in Jesus' name and on the basis of his indwelling words. Thus, whenever these conditions are met we can ask for whatever we wish and it will be ours. Accordingly, the author of 1 John tells us that "if our heart does not condemn us, we have confidence before God; and whatever we ask we receive from him, because we keep his commandments and do what pleases him" (1 John 3:21–22). Further, he tells us that if we "ask anything according to his will he hears us. And if we know that he hears us in whatever we ask, we know that we have the requests that we have asked of him" (1 John 5:14–15). Once again, upon meeting these conditions, the Johannine literature gives us good reasons to have confidence in prayer.

Accordingly, as noted in chapter 2 of this book, God has given his name to Jesus, and Jesus has, in turn, given believers permission to use his name in prayer. When we pray in his name we must be careful not to do so in a flippant, irreverent manner. Instead we should pray in a manner that honors the third commandment (Exod 20:7). Doing so involves praying in a manner that honors Jesus and the One who sent him. It means not tacking Jesus' name to the end of our prayer as a religious duty, but offering petitions in his name with joyful delight. Furthermore, honoring his name also involves showing esteem for it in our daily lives as we remain faithful to him and submit to his lordship. We cannot expect God to listen to our words to him in prayer if we ignore his words to us in sacred Scripture. Notwithstanding, as we remain faithful to Jesus, it is his good pleasure to answer our prayers.

The Posture of Prayer

As indicated in chapter 2, Johannine prayer is ethical insofar as it is motivated by love for God and the honor of his name above all else. But this sort of prayer also has horizontal implications for our fellow brothers and sisters in the local church. In this model, Johannine prayer is offered from a posture of humility and servanthood. As such, prayer should be offered on the basis of Jesus' loving example in washing his disciples' feet (John 13:15), and ultimately in him laying down his life for them in his cross-death (15:13). Modeled after these examples, prayer for others is one of the ways by which we love and serve them. Whether we stand or kneel, this sort of prayer is others-centered. It turns us inside out for the sake of the believing community and the unbelieving world. It seeks for the well-being of others and their fruitfulness. We should ask, If God answered our prayers, would they benefit anyone besides us? Even prayer for our own personal gain and spiritual growth should not be for our benefit alone. The more Christ-like we become the better we are equipped to serve others. In chapter 4 I argued that the Elder's prayer-wish for Gaius's prosperity was not for him alone but for the good of the emissaries under his care. As Gaius prospered, they, in turn, would be equipped and refreshed to carry forth the mission of God. Third John reminds us that it is not wrong to pray for physical prosperity as long as we remember that good health and material blessings should be used for the sake of being a blessing to others. In this paradigm, the things of this world are simply the means to the greater end of loving people and serving them in the way Jesus modeled for us.

Moreover, the author of 1 John reminds us that prayer serves as one of the means by which a sinning brother is restored to life (5:14–16). While it is impossible to be sure, perhaps he is thinking about someone in the believing community who has acted unethically toward a fellow believer. Whatever the case, we would do well to pray for those in the church who have drifted from God's ethical standards. Of course, there is a time to lovingly confront our brothers and sisters face-to-face about the sin they commit, but perhaps we should seek God's face in prayer before such confrontation takes place. In other words, we should view prayer as our first response instead of a last resort.

Furthermore, our love must also extend to the unbelieving world that Jesus died for. Although the FD does not explicitly tell us to pray for the salvation of the world, this is certainly the implication of prayer in Jesus' name. Given the meaning of his name ("Yahweh saves") and the nature of his saving mission (John 3:16), our prayers should center on the growth of the church and the advancement of the kingdom of God as more and more disciples are produced after Jesus' kind. This is the essence of Johannine prayer. It compels us to cry out for our communities, for our country, and even for entire continents that are covered in moral darkness. In the final analysis, it calls for the kingdom of this world to "become the kingdom of our Lord and of his Christ" (Rev 11:15).

The Perspective of Prayer

Finally, the book of Revelation provides an eschatological perspective for our prayers. That is, it helps us to see things on earth from the perspective of heaven and to pray accordingly. It justifies our prayer requests that wholeness of the future will break forth into the brokenness of our present situations. This sort of prayer not only calls for Jesus to come again in the future, it also summons forth his kingdom to invade our present lives. Stanley Grenz says, "Prayer is the cry for the Kingdom. In prayer, we address God who is willing and able to act. We petition God that the power of the future might break into the brokenness of the present. In this sense, to pray is to express our longing that the will of God be done on earth, as it is in heaven."[2] As noted in chapter 5 of this book, justification for eschatological prayers is found in Revelation wherein John tells us that the prayers of the saints ascended to the throne room in heaven before God (Rev 5:8; 8:3–4). While the exact details of what these prayers consisted of is not indicated

2. Grenz, *Prayer*, 54.

in the text, I have argued that these prayers likely involved petitions for both the continuation and the completion of the mission of God in the world. More specifically, it is likely that they called on God to vindicate those who have been slaughtered for their Christian witness. This was most certainly the cry of the martyrs in 6:10. Nevertheless the book of Revelation not only highlights the prayers of the righteous, it also outlines God's responses to them in acts of judgment and salvation. As such, Revelation provides two outcomes: the wicked are judged by the wrath of the Lamb and the righteous are saved by the blood of the Lamb (5:9; 6:16–17; 12:11; 14:10; 19:15). While acts of judgment and salvation will occur throughout history, these themes reach an appropriate climax at the second advent of Jesus. Therefore, as we wait upon his return, our prayer-cries should be modeled after the prayers of the saints and the martyrs. We should pray that God will vindicate those who have been oppressed and afflicted for the sake of the Gospel. We should pray that God will defend his honor among the nations. It is distinctively Johannine for us to long to see God's justice revealed in this world. But our central prayer-cry should be for the hostile enemies of the cross to become the reconciled friends of God.

Moreover, like the other Johannine literature, Revelation reminds us that God is faithful to answer prayer; but the answer comes in his timing, not in ours (6:11). And while we wait, we suffer. Our anticipation is often accompanied by fiery tribulation. Nevertheless, Revelation reminds us that our eschatological hopes may be delayed, but they will not be denied. God will have the final say in history. As such, the victorious outlook of Revelation should give us confidence in our present situation as we are in conflict with the Caesars of this world. Besides, our prayers are offered in the name of the King of kings and the Lord of lords (Rev 19:16). He is the one before whom the kings of the earth must bow. Thus, without ignoring the pain of this present world, our personal and corporate prayers should articulate a theology of victory. And since public prayer has didactic value, we should take advantage of every opportunity to pray in a manner that reflects our eschatological hopes. As we anticipate Jesus' second advent, we must realize that this world will always be a place of sin, sickness, and apparent setbacks. Restlessness, rebellion, and ruin will continue to mark our fallen world. Therefore, we look forward to a new heaven and a new earth as we cry out in prayer, "Amen. Come, Lord Jesus!" (Rev 21:1; 22:20).

Bibliography

Adams, Scott. "An Examination of Prayer in 3 John 2 and the Farewell Discourse in Light of the Mission of God." *Neotestamentica* 54 (2020) 187–207. doi:10.1353/neo.2020.0015.

———. "Prayer in the Farewell Discourse: An Exegetical Investigation." PhD diss., Radboud University, 2018.

———. "Prayer in Johannine Perspective: An Analysis of Prayer in the Farewell Discourse and 1 John." *Neotestamentica* 54 (2020) 105–28. doi:10.1353/neo.2020.0012.

———. *Prayer in John's Farewell Discourse: An Exegetical Investigation*. Eugene, OR: Pickwick, 2020.

———. "The Rhetorical Function of Petitionary Prayer in Revelation." *Neotestamentica* 55 (2021) 1–22. doi: 10.1353/neo.2021.0000.

Akin, Daniel L. *1, 2, 3 John: An Exegetical and Theological Exposition of the Holy Scripture*. The New American Commentary 38. Nashville: B&H, 2001.

Alexander, T. Desmond. *Exodus*. Edited by David W. Baker and Gordon J. Wenham. Apollos Old Testament Commentary 2. Downers Grove, IL: InterVarsity, 2017.

Ashton, John. *Understanding the Fourth Gospel*. Oxford: Clarendon, 1991.

Aune, David E. "Magic in Early Christianity." In *Aufstieg und Niedergang der römischen Welt Religion*, edited by Hildegard Temporini and Wolfgang Haase, 23/2:1507–57. Berlin: de Gruyter, 1980.

———. *Revelation 1–5*. Word Biblical Commentary 52A. Grand Rapids: Zondervan Academic, 1997. Kindle.

———. *Revelation 6–16*. Word Biblical Commentary 52B. Grand Rapids: Zondervan Academic, 1998. Kindle.

———. *Revelation 17–22*. Word Biblical Commentary 52C. Grand Rapids: Zondervan Academic, 2016. Kindle.

Barker, Margaret. *Revelation of Jesus Christ: Which God Gave to Him to Show to His Servants What Must Soon Take Place (Revelation 1.1)*. Edinburgh: T. & T. Clark, 2000.

Bibliography

Bauckham, Richard. "Prayer in the Book of Revelation." In *Into God's Presence: Prayer in the New Testament*, edited by Richard N. Longenecker, 252–70. Grand Rapids: Eerdmans, 2001.

Beale, G. K. *The Book of Revelation: A Commentary on the Greek Text*. New International Greek Testament Commentary. Grand Rapids: Eerdmans, 1999.

Beale, G. K., and David H. Campbell. *Revelation: A Shorter Commentary*. Grand Rapids: Eerdmans, 2015. Kindle.

Beasley-Murray, George R. *The Book of Revelation*. Eugene, OR: Wipf & Stock, 1981.

Beutler, Johannes. *A Commentary on the Gospel of John*. Translated by Michael Tait. Grand Rapids: Eerdmans, 2017.

Bilaniuk, Petro. "Some Remarks concerning a Theological Description of Prayer." *Greek Orthodox Theological Review* 21 (1976) 203–14.

Blount, Brian K. *Revelation: A Commentary*. Louisville: Westminster John Knox, 2009.

Bradshaw, Paul F. *Daily Prayer in the Early Church: A Study of the Origin and Early Development of the Divine Office*. London: SPCK, 1981.

Brown, Raymond E. *The Epistles of John*. Anchor Bible 30. Garden City, NY: Doubleday, 1982.

———. *The Gospel according to John (XIII–XXI)*. Anchor Bible 29A. Garden City, NY: Doubleday, 1970.

Brown, Sherri, and Christopher W. Skinner. *Johannine Ethics: The Moral World of the Gospel and Epistles of John*. Minneapolis: Fortress, 2017.

Bruce, F. F. *The Gospel and Epistles of John*. Grand Rapids: Eerdmans, 1983.

Bultmann, Rudolf. *The Johannine Epistles: A Commentary on the Johannine Epistles*. Edited by Robert Funk. Translated by R. Philip O'Hara et al. Hermeneia. Philadelphia: Fortress, 1973.

Carson, D. A. *The Farewell Discourse and Final Prayer of Jesus: An Exposition of John 14–17*. Grand Rapids: Baker Book House, 1980.

———. *The Gospel according to John*. Pillar New Testament Commentary. Grand Rapids: Eerdmans, 1991.

Charles, R. H., ed. and trans. *The Testaments of the Twelve Patriarchs: Translation*. London: Adam and Charles Black, 1908.

Charlesworth, James H., ed., with Mark Harding and Mark Kiley. *The Lord's Prayer and Other Prayer Texts from the Greco-Roman Era*. Valley Forge, PA: Trinity Press International, 1994.

Crump, David. *Knocking on Heaven's Door: A New Testament Theology of Petitionary Prayer*. Grand Rapids: Baker Academic, 2006.

Cullmann, Oscar. *Das Gebet im Neuen Testament: Zugleich Versuch einer vom Neuen Testament aus zu erteilenden Antwort auf heutige Fragen*. 2nd ed. Tübingen: Mohr Siebeck, 1997.

———. *Early Christian Worship*. Translated by A. Stewart Todd and James B. Torrance. Studies in Biblical Theology. London: SCM, 1969.

Culpepper, R. Alan. *The Gospel and Letters of John*. Nashville: Abingdon, 1998.

Bibliography

Culpepper, R. Alan, and Paul N. Anderson, eds. *Communities in Dispute: Current Scholarship on the Johannine Epistles*. Atlanta: Society of Biblical Literature, 2014.

Danker, Frederick W., et al. *Greek-English Lexicon of the New Testament and Other Early Christian Literature*. 3rd ed. Chicago: University of Chicago Press, 2000.

Derickson, Gary W. *First, Second, and Third John*. Edited by H. Wayne House et al. Evangelical Exegetical Commentary. Bellingham, WA: Lexham, 2012.

DeSilva, David A. *Seeing Things John's Way: The Rhetoric of the Book of Revelation*. Louisville: Westminster John Knox, 2009.

Dodd, C. H. *The Interpretation of the Fourth Gospel*. Cambridge: Cambridge University Press, 1953.

Dozeman, Thomas B. *Commentary on Exodus*. Eerdmans Critical Commentary. Grand Rapids: Eerdmans, 2009.

Fee, Gordon D. *Revelation*. New Covenant Commentary Series. Eugene, OR: Cascade, 2011.

Funk, Robert W. "The Form and Structure of II and III John." *Journal of Biblical Literature* 86 (1967) 424–30. doi:10.2307/3262797.

Giesen, Heinz. *Die Offenbarung des Johannes*. Regensburger New Testament. Regensburg: Pustet, 1997.

Gonzalez, Martin Fontenot, ed. *The Didache, or Teaching of the Twelve Apostles*. Translated by Charles H. Hoole. https://pages.uoregon.edu/sshoemak/321/texts/didache.html.

Gorman, Michael J. "John's Implicit Ethic of Enemy-Love." In *Johannine Ethics: The Moral World of the Gospel and Epistles and John*, edited by Sherri Brown and Christopher W. Skinner, 135–58. Minneapolis: Fortress, 2017.

Graf, Fritz. "Prayer in Magic and Religious Ritual." In *Magika Hiera: Ancient Greek Magic and Religion*, edited by Christopher A. Faraone and Dirk Obbink, 188–213. New York: Oxford University Press, 1997.

Grenz, Stanley. *Prayer: The Cry for the Kingdom*. Grand Rapids: Eerdmans, 2005.

Hays, Richard B. *The Moral Vision of the New Testament: A Contemporary Introduction to New Testament Ethics*. New York: HarperOne, 1996.

Hunter, W. Bingham. "The Prayers of Jesus in the Gospel of John." PhD diss., University of Aberdeen, 1979.

Hurtado, Larry W. *Lord Jesus Christ: Devotion to Jesus in Earliest Christianity*. Grand Rapids: Eerdmans, 2003.

Imes, Carmen Joy. *Bearing God's Name: Why Sinai Still Matters*. Downers Grove, IL: InterVarsity, 2019.

Janowitz, Naomi. *Magic in the Roman World: Pagans, Jews, and Christians*. London: Routledge, 2001.

Jeffers, James S. *The Greco-Roman World of the New Testament Era: Exploring the Background of Early Christianity*. Downers Grove, IL: InterVarsity, 1999.

Jeremias, Joachim. *The Prayers of Jesus*. London: SCM, 1967.

Bibliography

Jobes, Karen H. *1, 2, & 3 John*. Edited by Clinton E. Arnold. Zondervan Exegetical Commentary on the New Testament. Grand Rapids: Zondervan, 2014.

Kaiser, Walter C., Jr. "Exodus." In *The Expositor's Bible Commentary: Genesis–Leviticus*, edited by Tremper Longman III and David E. Garland, 1:333–562. Grand Rapids: Zondervan, 2008.

Kanagaraj, Jey J. "The Implied Ethics of the Fourth Gospel: A Reinterpretation of the Decalogue." *Tyndale Bulletin* 52 (2001) 33–60. https://tyndalebulletin.org/article/30259-the-implied-ethics-of-the-fourth-gospel-a-reinterpretation-of-the-decalogue.

Karakolis, Christos. "Semeia Conveying Ethics in the Gospel according to John." In *Rethinking the Ethics of John: "Implicit Ethics" in the Johannine Writings*, edited by Jan G. van der Watt and Ruben Zimmermann, 192–212. Wissenschaftliche Untersuchungen zum Neuen Testament 291. Tübingen: Mohr Siebeck, 2012.

Karris, Robert J. *Prayer and the New Testament: Jesus and His Communities at Worship*. New York: Crossroad, 2000.

Keener, Craig S. *The Gospel of John*. 2 vols. Peabody, MA: Hendrickson, 2003.

———. *Revelation*. The NIV Application Commentary. Grand Rapids: Zondervan, 2002.

Kiley, Mark, ed. *Prayer from Alexander to Constantine: A Critical Anthology*. London: Routledge, 1997.

Kittel, Gerhard, and Gerhard Friedrich, eds. *Theological Dictionary of the New Testament*. Translated and edited by Geoffrey W. Bromiley. Grand Rapids: Eerdmans, 1985.

Klauck, Hans-Josef. *The Religious Context of Early Christianity: A Guide to Graeco-Roman Religions*. Translated by Brian McNeil. Minneapolis: Fortress, 2003.

Klein, Hans, et al., eds. *Das Gebet im Neuen Testament: Vierte europäische orthodox-westliche Exegetenkonferenz in Sâmbăta de Sus, 4.–8. August 2007*. Wissenschaftliche Untersuchungen zum Neuen Testament 249. Tübingen: Mohr Siebeck, 2009.

Koester, Craig R. "Rethinking the Ethics of John: A Review Article." *Journal for the Study of the New Testament* 36 (2013) 85–98. doi:10.1177/0142064X13495133.

———. *Revelation*. Anchor Yale Bible 38A. New Haven: Yale University Press, 2014.

Köstenberger, Andreas J. *Encountering John: The Gospel in Historical, Literary, and Theological Perspective*. Encountering Biblical Studies. Grand Rapids: Baker Academic, 2002.

———. *A Theology of John's Gospel and Letters: The Word, the Christ, the Son of God*. Biblical Theology of the New Testament. Grand Rapids: Zondervan, 2009.

Kruse, Colin G. *The Letters of John*. Pillar New Testament Commentary. Grand Rapids: Eerdmans, 2000.

BIBLIOGRAPHY

Labahn, Michael. "'It's Only Love'—Is That All? Limits and Potentials of Johannine 'Ethic'—A Critical Evaluation of Research." In *Rethinking the Ethics of John: "Implicit Ethics" in the Johannine Writings*, edited by Jan G. van der Watt and Ruben Zimmermann, 3–43. Wissenschaftliche Untersuchungen zum Neuen Testament 291. Tübingen: Mohr Siebeck, 2012.

Ladd, George Eldon. *A Commentary on the Revelation of John*. Grand Rapids: Eerdmans, 1972.

Lenksi, R. C. H. *The Interpretation of I and II Epistles of Peter, the Three Epistles of John, and the Epistle of Jude*. Minneapolis: Augsburg, 1966.

Lieu, Judith M. "The Audience of the Johannine Epistles." In *Communities in Dispute: Current Scholarship on the Johannine Epistles*, edited by R. Alan Culpepper and Paul N. Anderson, 123–40. Atlanta: Society of Biblical Literature, 2014.

———. *I, II, & III John: A Commentary*. The New Testament Library. Louisville: Westminster John Knox, 2008.

Loader, William R. G. "The Law and Ethics in John's Gospel." In *Rethinking the Ethics of John: "Implicit Ethics" in the Johannine Writings*, edited by Jan G. van der Watt and Ruben Zimmermann, 143–58. Wissenschaftliche Untersuchungen zum Neuen Testament 291. Tübingen: Mohr Siebeck, 2012.

Longenecker, Richard N. *Into God's Presence: Prayer in the New Testament*. Grand Rapids: Eerdmans, 2001.

Malherbe, Abraham J. *Social Aspects of Early Christianity*. 2nd ed. Eugene, OR: Wipf & Stock, 2003.

Marshall, I. Howard. *The Epistles of John*. Grand Rapids: Eerdmans, 1978.

Michaels, J. Ramsey. "Finding Yourself an Intercessor: New Testament Prayer from Hebrews to Jude." In *Into God's Presence: Prayer in the New Testament*, edited by Richard N. Longenecker, 228–51. Grand Rapids: Eerdmans, 2001.

Middleton, Paul. *The Violence of the Lamb: Martyrs as Agents of Divine Judgment in the Book of Revelation*. Library of New Testament Studies. London: T. & T. Clark, 2018.

Moloney, Francis J. *The Apocalypse of John: A Commentary*. Grand Rapids: Baker Academic, 2020.

———. *Glory Not Dishonor: Reading John 13–21*. Minneapolis: Fortress, 1998.

———. *Love in the Gospel of John: An Exegetical, Theological, and Literary Study*. Grand Rapids: Baker Academic, 2013.

Morris, Leon L. *Revelation: An Introduction and Commentary*. Tyndale New Testament Commentaries 20. Downers Grove, IL: InterVarsity, 1987.

Mounce, Robert H. *The Book of Revelation*. The New International Commentary on the New Testament. Grand Rapids: Eerdmans, 1997. Kindle.

Nestle, Eberhard, et al., eds. *Novum Testamentum Graece*. 27th ed. Stuttgart: Deutsche Bibelgesellschaft, 1993.

BIBLIOGRAPHY

Neyrey, Jerome H. *Give God the Glory: Ancient Prayer and Worship in Cultural Perspective*. Grand Rapids: Eerdmans, 2007.

Neyrey, Jerome. H., and Eric C. Stewart, eds. *The Social World of the New Testament: Insights and Models*. Peabody, MA: Hendrickson, 2008.

Ng, Esther Yue L. "Prayer in Revelation." In *Teach Us to Pray: Prayer in the Bible and the World*, edited by D. A. Carson, 119–35. 1990. Reprint, Eugene, OR: Wipf & Stock, 2002.

Osborne, Grant R. *Revelation*. Baker Exegetical Commentary on the New Testament. Grand Rapids: Baker Academic, 2002.

Ostmeyer, Karl-Heinrich. *Kommunikation mit Gott und Christus: Sprache und Theologie des Gebetes im Neuen Testament*. Edited by Jörg Frey. Wissenschaftliche Untersuchungen zum Neuen Testament 197. Tübingen: Mohr Siebeck, 2006.

———. "Prayer as Demarcation: The Function of Prayer in the Gospel of John." In *Das Gebet im Neuen Testament: Vierte europäische orthodox-westliche Exegetenkonferenz in Sâmbata de Sus, 4.–8. August 2007*, edited by Hans Klein et al., 233–47. Wissenschaftliche Untersuchungen zum Neuen Testament 249. Tübingen: Mohr Siebeck, 2009.

Painter, John. *1, 2, and 3 John*. Edited by Daniel J. Harrington. Sacra Pagina 18. Collegeville, MN: Liturgical, 2002.

Patterson, Paige. *Revelation*. The New American Commentary 39. Nashville: B&H Academic, 2012.

Penner, Jeremy. *Patterns of Daily Prayer in Second Temple Period Judaism*. Edited by Florentino García Martínez. Studies on the Texts of the Desert of Judah 104. Leiden: Brill, 2012.

Peterson, David G. "Prayer in the General Epistles." In *Teach Us to Pray: Prayer in the Bible and the World*, edited by D. A. Carson, 84–101. 1990. Reprint, Eugene, OR: Wipf & Stock, 2002.

Philo of Alexandria. *The Works of Philo: Complete and Unabridged*. Translated by C. D. Yonge. Peabody: Hendrickson, 1995.

Rainbow, Paul A. *Johannine Theology: The Gospels, the Epistles, and the Apocalypse*. Downers Grove, IL: InterVarsity, 2014.

Ruiz, Jean-Pierre. "Revelation 4:8–11; 5:9–14: Heavenly Hymns of Creation and Redemption." In *Prayer from Alexander to Constantine: A Critical Anthology*, edited by Mark Kiley, 244–49. London: Routledge, 1997.

Sanders, Jack T. *Ethics in the New Testament: Change and Development*. Philadelphia: Fortress, 1975.

Schnackenburg, Rudolf. *The Gospel according to St. John*. Vol. 3, *Commentary on Chapters 13–21*. Translated by David Smith and G. A. Kon. New York: Crossroad, 1982.

———. *The Johannine Epistles: Introduction and Commentary*. Translated by Reginald and Ilse Fuller. New York: Crossroad, 1992.

Skinner, Christopher W. "(How) Can We Talk about Johannine Ethic? Looking Back and Moving Forward." In *Johannine Ethics: The Moral World of the*

BIBLIOGRAPHY

Gospel and Epistles and John, edited by Sherri Brown and Christopher W. Skinner, xvii–xix. Minneapolis: Fortress, 2017

———. "Love One Another: The Johannine Love Command in the Farewell Discourse." In *Johannine Ethics: The Moral World of the Gospel and Epistles and John*, edited by Sherri Brown and Christopher W. Skinner, 25–42. Minneapolis: Fortress, 2017.

Smalley, Stephen S. *1, 2, 3 John*. World Biblical Commentary 51. Dallas: Word, 1984.

———. *The Revelation to John: A Commentary on the Greek Text of the Apocalypse*. Downers Grove, IL: InterVarsity, 2005.

Smith. D. Moody. *First, Second, and Third John*. Interpretation, a Bible Commentary for Teaching and Preaching. Louisville: Westminster John Knox, 2012.

Stevick, Daniel B. *Jesus and His Own: A Commentary on John 13–17*. Eerdmans: Grand Rapids, 2011.

Stott, John. *The Epistles of John*. The Tyndale New Testament Commentaries. Grand Rapids: Eerdmans, 1964.

Strecker, Georg. *The Johannine Letters: A Commentary on 1, 2, and 3 John*. Edited by Harold W. Attridge. Translated by Linda M. Maloney. Hermeneia—A Critical and Historical Commentary on the Bible. Minneapolis: Fortress, 1996.

Stuart, Douglas K. *Exodus*. New American Commentary 2. Nashville: Broadman & Holman, 2006.

Stuhlmacher, Peter. *Biblical Theology of the New Testament*. Edited and translated by Daniel P. Bailey. Grand Rapids: Eerdmans, 2018.

Tabb, Brian J. *All Things New: Revelation as Canonical Capstone*. New Studies in Biblical Theology. London: Apollos, 2019.

Thatcher, Tom. *3 John*. In *The Expositor's Bible Commentary: Hebrews-Revelation*, edited by Tremper Longman III and David E. Garland, 13:525–38. Grand Rapids: Zondervan, 2006.

Thomas, John Christopher, and Frank Macchia. *Revelation*. The Two Horizons New Testament Commentary. Grand Rapids: Eerdmans, 2016. Kindle.

Trudinger, Paul. "Concerning Sins, Mortal and Otherwise: A Note on 1 John 5,16–17." *Biblica* 52 (1971) 541–42.

Van der Watt, Jan G. "Ethics and Ethos in the Gospel according to John." *Zeitschrift Für Die Neutestamentliche Wissenschaft Und Die Kunde Der Älteren Kirche* 97 (2006) 147–76. doi:10.1515/ZNTW.2006.012.

———. *Family of the King: Dynamics of Metaphor in the Gospel according to John*. Biblical Interpretation Series 47. Leiden: Brill, 2000. eBook.

———. *An Introduction to the Johannine Gospels and Letters*. T. & T. Clark Approaches to Biblical Studies. London: T. & T. Clark, 2007.

———. "Mimesis or Imitation in Ethical Dynamics." Lecture, Radboud University, Nijmegen, Netherlands, December 2014.

Van der Watt, Jan G., and Ruben Zimmermann, eds. *Rethinking the Ethics of John: "Implicit Ethics" in the Johannine Writings*. Wissenschaftliche

Untersuchungen zum Neuen Testament 291. Tübingen: Mohr Siebeck, 2012.

Von Wahlde, Urban C. *The Gospel and Letters of John.* Vol. 3, *Commentary on the Three Johannine Letters.* Eerdmans Critical Commentary. Grand Rapids: Eerdmans, 2010.

———. "Raymond Brown's View of the Crisis of 1 John: In the Light of Some Peculiar Features of the Johannine Gospel." In *Communities in Dispute: Current Scholarship on the Johannine Epistles,* edited by R. Alan Culpepper and Paul N. Anderson, 19–46. Atlanta: Society of Biblical Literature, 2014.

Westcott, Brooke Foss. *The Epistles of St. John: The Greek Text with Notes and Essays.* 2nd ed. 1886. Reprint, Eugene, OR: Wipf & Stock, 2001.

Weyer-Menkhoff, Karl. "The Response of Jesus: Ethics in John by Considering Scripture as Work of God." In *Rethinking the Ethics of John: "Implicit Ethics" in the Johannine Writings,* edited by Jan G. van der Watt and Ruben Zimmermann, 159–74. Wissenschaftliche Untersuchungen zum Neuen Testament 291. Tübingen: Mohr Siebeck, 2012.

Witherington, Ben, III. *John's Wisdom: A Commentary on the Fourth Gospel.* Louisville: Westminster John Knox, 1995.

———. *Revelation.* The New Cambridge Bible Commentary. New York: Cambridge University Press, 2003.

Yarbrough, Robert W. *1–3 John.* Baker Exegetical Commentary on the New Testament. Grand Rapids: Baker Academic, 2008.

www.ingramcontent.com/pod-product-compliance
Lightning Source LLC
Chambersburg PA
CBHW070932160426
43193CB00011B/1663